VisionFactory: Adventures in Corpo

A veteran producer's guide to corporate video production from script to screen

Steven D. White

Acknowledgements: This book would not have been possible without the help of my fellow VisionFactory colleagues: Michael Worthington, Deven Spear, John Pugh, Eric Jones, Meri Kotlas, Dan Lott, and many others. I'd also like to thank my family, Davida, Bronwyn, Elijah, Jamie, Sage and Indiana for their support.

This book is dedicated to my mother, Judy Adams White who kicked cancer's ass as I sat writing the first pages by her bedside.

First Edition - Published by Steve White Productions, Asheville, NC

Cover: Based on Art created by Meri Kotlas.

Additional Art by: Eric Jones, James Maxx Andersen

Printed in the United States of America

ISBN-13: 978-1494789503
ISBN-10: 1494789507
BISAC: Performing Arts / Film & Video / Screenwriting

Table of Contents

Preface:

My favorite film of all time is what I call Crayon Film. It's the short movie that most people have seen on Sesame Street depicting the manufacture of a crayon as shown through a series of shots on a factory floor. It was shot on film sometime in the early 70's and holds up to this day as a perfectly crafted work of art. The film is beautifully shot and edited, and set to a wonderful synthesized piece of music. The story is simple – kid looks at a crayon, we see how a crayon is made, back to the kid, the end. It's the execution that makes it so amazing. The subject matter is always moving and progressing, developing into a final completion. It's circular, complete, colorful, perfectly paced, and fun. It never gets old to me.

For many reasons, I like to think about Crayon Film when working on a project, especially during editing and often while shooting. Come to think of it, even when writing, I think Crayon Film is a big motivator because of its simplicity. There is a natural structure to the story, and the filmmaker's job is to get to that structure as naturally as possible.

I have always been interested in film and video, from my first experiments with a silent Super-8 film camera to producing and directing a feature film, and over 15 years as a working producer in corporate media. Over this time the tools of the trade have evolved dramatically, empowering a new generation of film and video artists, and creating many exciting avenues to make a business out of video and interactive media production.

This book is about exploring these possibilities through actual practical examples of scripts and the productions that were created from them. The text will be heavy on the script side. I'm choosing this approach because I don't know of many resources that use actually produced corporate scripts to help teach a practical approach to production. I also am choosing this route because I don't consider myself to be necessarily an expert writer or an expert producer. But what I am capable of doing is showing the real world examples of projects that I created or helped to create and share some insights on what went well and what didn't. Hopefully the fact that all of the examples in the book are works that were created for paying clients will give you a nice roadmap on how you might go about creating similar work. Perhaps you'll learn some things to avoid along the way as well.

What I am hoping to create with this project is the kind of resource that would have helped me when I was starting out as a corporate producer. If I succeed, then this will act as a primer for a variety of professional situations and different types of productions that you might find as a corporate producer. It might help you avoid "making it up as you go", which was the norm for the beginning of my career. I also hope to shed some light on the process involved in creating a video from the first client contact, to the delivery of a finished master. After producing for many years I realize that the act of creation involves several important things. Among these there are three essential elements that come to mind: art, craft and finesse. Art refers to creating something new, unique, and engaging. Craft refers to the methodologies that allow you to create with quality and efficiency. And finesse refers to the art and craft of dealing with people while doing the other two. Each element is crucial to producing a successful piece of media for a client, and it all begins with the script stage.

Some background: I began working for a small four person video company in 1995 after completing an independent feature film. The company was called Digital Imagery and was started by two employees of Nortel, a tech company famous for creating the digital telephone switch. Nortel, formerly known as Northern Telecom, was a giant in telecom technology and, like many other communications manufacturers at the time, they were beginning to develop and refine the infrastructure for the Internet. This was a very competitive field during the mid to late 90's, with other giants like HP, Lucent, and Cisco aggressively investing in new technology and services. Fortunately for our small company, this meant a nice flow of marketing dollars to promote these products and companies.

The mid-nineties brought about a real shift in the media world. Interactive media was becoming more common in the form of Macromedia Director projects, Web Sites, and a variety of fairly expensive interactive kiosks. Non-linear editing was becoming an affordable alternative to expensive offline and online tape-based editing suites. And perhaps most significantly, digital video cameras like Sony's VX-1000 were creating a level playing field between young upstart producers and video veterans.

Having worked previously for some more experienced video producers, I realized that the new technology was a game changer. The cameras were lighter. The quality was as good or better. The batteries lasted longer, and best of all, it was cheaper. The advent of DV-CAM, and other mini-DV based cameras meant no loss in image quality during editing, cheaper tape costs, and a very agile platform for a new wave of production.

Quickly, our small company began to attract attention because we were driven by innovation and began developing what were then cutting edge solutions by using these new tools. We also found a wealth of new software tools to help create the customer's vision. These included Cosa's (later Adobe's) After Effects, Media-100 non-linear editors, Macromedia's Director and Authorware, and many other essentials like Photoshop, Media Cleaner Pro, and variety of shareware tools. Sometimes if we needed a tool, we'd invent it or work with a developer to make something special.

The first few projects for Digital Imagery included a promotional video for a modeling agency, some digital enhancements of old video tapes and a piece called "Busy as a

Bee". The latter was a short internal marketing video for a division of Nortel that could serve as a template for many productions to come.

"Busy as a Bee" was a celebration of the efforts of employees in many different North American Cities. It was a fluff piece for internal consumption, didn't have a huge budget, but did include some travel for on location shoots. My boss Michael Worthington shot the footage, my new co-worker Eric Jones animated the effects, and I edited the piece. Together, we were able to craft a mix of animation, camera work, music and narration to create a whimsical short film. The 2d animation done in After Effects on an ancient Mac desktop was pure cheese, but still perfectly effective. The fast motion sunset over the factory in Calgary looked way more expensive than it really was, and the same high speed effect on busy company workers was a huge success. Mix in 'Flight of the Bumblebee" and the quickly paced video cut on the Media-100 was a fresh, high-end looking piece delivered on a budget. The same effects heavy video, even one year before, would have cost ten times as much at a traditional post facility.

There are many things I learned from the experience of working on "Busy as a Bee". The first was that people actually paid for creating something basically silly. The story was simple - everybody is running around really fast doing stuff, good for them. It was punctuated with silly visual devices and MTV pacing, and had a feeling of "production value". It was exactly what the client wanted, a clever ego boost for all of the drones, and they paid to get it. Another thing I learned was that if we could think of an idea, we could also find a way to create it. The animated bees that still make me laugh today were made up of about 30 layers of an After Effects project, each bee completing its own spastic path across the screen. Our animator and quick learner of every software package he ever opened, Eric Jones, pushed the Mac to the limit with each new spastic bee.

That idea of "layers" was perhaps the most important thing I took from this the process, not just layers of graphics in After Effects or on a timeline in the Media-100, but the idea of "layers of production". Each small element that went into the final piece started in another form, sometimes on a different machine. All of the live video was captured and altered in some way, the animation was made up of layers that were created in illustrator or Photoshop, and the rendered elements were then imported into the timeline. This was unlike any kind of production I had been involved with before. It was more akin to Walt Disney than to Crayon Film.

Another thing I learned from my early days at Digital Imagery was the power of working with a team of uniquely qualified people. I began as an editor and found myself working with a versatile animator and technologist - the previously mentioned Eric Jones, or Dr. Jones as we called him, a talented videographer, producer and writer - my boss Michael Worthington, a musician and tech expert – John Pugh, a world class graphic design artist - Meri Kotlas, a talented interactive programmer – Dan Lott, and a visionary thinker who loved to build impossible things (and sell them) – Deven Spear . We were all young and essentially geeks in the grandest mid-nineties sense of the word, raised on different 1980's home computers, arcade games, Star Wars and Tron.

After a few months of success working from a small garage in Durham, NC we moved into our first offices in Research Triangle Park (RTP), North Carolina's answer to Silicon Valley, and changed our name to VisionFactory. Despite being confused for a glasses manufacturer, VisionFactory soon gained a reputation for creating a dynamic mix of interactivity, digital video and creative design. The Nortel marketing leads began to take notice, and they had a growing number of stories to tell and the budgets to tell them.

We had a growing team of media artists and the unique ability to turn work around quickly. It was a good time to be in interactive media, and the company grew rapidly between the mid to late 90s. At its peak, VisionFactory had 55 employees and had branched from media production into interactive space design and content delivery product development. But media and video in particular were still at the heart of what brought us business. More specifically, it was our ability to deliver high production value content within interactive environments.

That was then.

Jumping ahead nearly 20 years after I started working in digital media, the technology has grown exponentially, and the talent base has also grown. Interactive media has blossomed due to the ubiquity of broadband internet, the continued cost drops in hardware and the cultural revolution riding the backs of innovations like Youtube, Facebook, and Twitter. Online media is becoming the first place that people look for information. Sharing is arguably more effective than paid advertising. This new landscape is a rich for media producers, allowing even the smallest business to affordably reach a wide audience. This means more customers wanting to tell their stories. For a video producer, it means a new market for creating and selling content. Where most of my productions in the 1990's were delivered on DVD or location based installations, today the delivery is almost exclusively online. Sites like Youtube, Vimeo, Blip.tv, and Brightcove all offer powerful streaming platforms that in most cases are free to use. This means getting content up and out quickly and embedding it on a client site or emailing links instantly.

These new technologies, and more innovations to come, mean that producers have the ability to distribute their products rapidly and to a potentially enormous audience. Clients have new ways to reach their customers. But the free availability of these tools also means the competition has the same reach and convenience to distribute. If you are becoming a producer today, differentiation is still an uphill battle. But one thing hasn't changed – you must still develop a rapport with a client, create something that tells their story the way they want it told, and stay within budget. If you can do that, then you can be a successful producer in the corporate world.

Chapter 1: FADE IN
How I got started in corporate video

As many careers in video begin, mine started as a lowly production assistant, grip, and sometime camera operator for an established corporate producer. Starting in the late 1980's this job consisted of carrying heavy lights, stands, reflector cards, tripods, camera cases, battery chargers and tons of batteries. This was the time of huge video cameras often tethered to a separate recording desk by a trunk of wires. Some productions used ¾ inch video tapes and others used more advanced Betacam. The work was hard, inelegant, and slow.

Editing was done on an offline edit system usually consisting of a slave deck to play back footage, an edit controller and a master deck to assemble the final cut. Most small productions were limited to video cuts only and two audio tracks which were primarily used for a dialogue track and a music bed. Once a fine cut was reached, the final master might be assembled in an expensive online session where multiple source decks could be used and effects such as dissolves, wipes, and over-laid graphics could be applied. This was accomplished by the editor controller using timecodes to rewind and precisely position the tapes, begin playing and at exactly the right time, record the clip to the master. The repeated in a whirl of mechanical ballet until the final track was laid and the master was complete. Not only did this process limit the creativity of the editor to a few basic techniques, it was also very expensive.

As I think back to these early days of production, one thing comes to mind, dinosaurs. These huge, clunky machines made for very little flexibility. Physical production was always a challenge, limiting the amount of shot variety, number of locations, and camera movements. Production also required more crew and made it difficult to shoot in small spaces. As a grip, it was my job to keep things moving as quickly as possible so that the director could concentrate on getting the footage he was after. The particular producer/director I worked with most often liked to use as much equipment as possible even on the smallest projects. I think it was his way of showing the client they were getting their money's worth. In reality they often got scratched walls, blown circuit breakers and messed up carpets. But they did get good lighting and solid work. I got a sore back from unloading and loading a cargo van full of equipment.

The first few productions I worked on were for a company that owned several hospitals. My boss had a long relationship with the company and they were updating some of their marketing materials. All of our shoots were on location at different facilities including a couple of hospitals, a mobile surgery trailer and some smaller offices. This made for several paid days as a grip for me, and I was able to absorb the production process as I went along. I soon learned that on a small crew, everybody ends up doing everything. I would hold a reflector card for hours, operate the boom mic, run the camera deck, and occasionally get to operate the camera. When the camera was not tethered to AC power, I would have to constantly shuttle batteries back and forth to the camera deck, with some lasting a whopping 15 minutes before needed to be recharged. Weighing about 10 pounds each, these were called bricks for a good reason.

On these shoots I learned a lot about how a camera crew is treated by almost everyone – they bend over backwards to help you. They allow you to go places that no one else is allowed, and when you are lucky, they feed you. On one location, the mobile surgery trailer, the director suited up in scrubs and was allowed to film a live surgery. I declined to go in on that one.

Another thing I learned was how people change when in front of the camera, especially during a one-on-one interview. Some people are completely natural and comfortable having a discussion with an off camera interviewer and others seem calm enough at first and then freeze the moment the tape starts to roll. I never really understood this sudden change until it happened to me years later when I did a formal interview about the company I was working for. This deer in the headlights stare and accompanying sweat can ruin a shoot, but I've found that even the worst interview can still yield some good usable clips. I've spent many years trying to master my interviewing technique to put everyone at ease, sometimes even rolling camera early and just conversing with the subject hoping to catch some nice responses before the pressure of the red light comes into play.

Having worked on some short films and volunteered on a couple of independent features, I had a sense of how a production was pieced together from a script. I had a basic understanding of how a scene was setup, how camera angles helped to give the editor enough coverage and how sound was captured. On these corporate shoots, there wasn't so much a script, but rather an outline and lists of questions. We would hit a location, conduct some headshot interviews and then shoot a ton of b-roll, the term for the non-dialogue footage from the location. The b-roll was literally shot on a second or "b" tape so it could be easily inserted in during the edit session over assembled interview clips which were shot on their own "a" tape.

Though these productions were essentially marketing pieces with strictly rigid messages and targeted audiences, there was still an element of documentary about them. There was some flexibility to create something interesting and unique, and the outline approach kept us looking for the best footage and interviews to fill in the story. Compared to continuity storytelling from the movies, this was a completely different animal.

I slowly moved from grip to camera operator and then eventually to editor before branching out on my own and seeking my own clients. One of the first corporate projects that I edited was on one of the first generation of non-linear computer based editors, a Media-100. Non-linear meant the ability to break away from cuts only edits and expensive online sessions. It made the process of assembling a production much more fluid. Suddenly we could try something to see if it worked, and tweak and try again. We could go from shot to shot with incredible ease and layer graphics and audio tracks. Playback was in real-time and the Media-100 offered some color effects and plenty of transitions. This evolution in technology opened up the possibilities of production. Techniques formerly limited only to the upper echelon of production houses were suddenly at our fingertips. The flexibility meant the ability to offer clients a new level of quality, and a certain "Wow" factor.

The emergence of non-linear editing systems corresponded with more sophisticated tools for design, video compositing, and audio mixing and effects. Tools like Photoshop and After Effects allowed the producer to create precise layered effects, surpassing what even Hollywood had done before. Incorporating these tools with the power of a non-linear timeline made it possible to create corporate media on a budget for a clientele used to paying much more for similar work. As a result, those producers set in their ways, with dinosaur equipment, found a new wave of competition.

As one of these new wave of producers, I found that the tools I began to use were actually less expensive, produced higher quality, and allowed production to flow much faster. The three things said impossible to coexist in business – Faster, Cheaper and Better – were all right there. Since the cameras were much lighter and required less light, shooting on location was much simpler. Integrating a variety of content through simple graphics and different animation techniques was also feasible. Additionally, incorporating footage from legacy projects was much easier once it was captured as a digital file. In fact, some of my early projects were simple reworks of existing footage or sexing up of things like PowerPoint projects. Having the flexibility of digital tools made almost anything possible.

When I joined the team at VisionFactory I soon realized that the enthusiasm for these new capabilities was also shared by our clients. I found a good project usually came from a client who was a producer at heart, bringing a ton of good ideas and personal interest in creating something fresh or groundbreaking. When we were able to earn the trust of a client and deliver something that exceeded their expectations, they always came back for more, often with a larger project.

Projects would become more and more modular, being completed in segments, and that segmentation would later naturally lead to rich interactivity. In fact, this approach became a selling point for the company for "foot in the door" sorts of projects. We could start with something small, gain the client's confidence, and then move to the next level.

My career as an editor, scriptwriter, director and producer benefitted from several lucky breaks. The opportunities presented themselves at the right time, and the team I worked with latched onto each one and tried our best to over deliver with each finished piece. The timing was right since the mid to late 90's was a period of rapid growth in communications technologies. We benefitted from intense marketing in digital telephony, networking and internet technology, capturing some very lucrative contracts for media and digital space development. Our relationship with Nortel was crucial to our early success and then we were able to branch out to many other clients based on that early work. Work for companies like Cisco, HP, IBM, Unisys, Bowe Bell and Howell, Sun Microsystems, EDS, and many others could be directly traced back to the pieces we created for Nortel.

It was a time of real 90 hour weeks, high pressure deadlines, wrestling with temperamental software and hardware tools, dealing with a finicky culture of creative people and producing an enormous amount of work. In short, it was a great time.

I hope in the following pages some of my personal excitement during that time comes through in the descriptions and examples of this book. Like I said before, all of these examples were created by working closely with paying clients. Each served its specific purpose. Some may seem silly, some dense, some might have been right on. In all the cases, they were the work of a versatile team of dedicated digital artists at a time when that term was just starting to be defined.

Chapter 2: The Role of the Script

The script is the backbone of any media project. It not only tells the story as it is to be seen or experienced by the viewer, it also acts as a guideline for every member of the production process. It is simply the single most critical document to the production. Whether the project is a product video, interactive kiosk, flash animation or computer game, the script is the overarching source of all of the production work. Every decision involving casting, sets, graphic design, sound design, interactivity, locations, camera angles, camera movement, 2D and 3D animation, graphical interfaces, and delivery method should be covered in detail on the written pages of the script.

With this understanding of the importance of the script, the producer must find a way to cram all of the needed information into document, while still keeping it easy to understand for the team and the client. For a traditional narrative video, this can be pretty straight forward. The script is made up of scenes that contain both description and dialogue and sometimes a little camera direction. When a script like this is well written, the act of reading it is much like experiencing the story as it is finally shown. For an interactive project, things get a bit trickier. The very nature of an interactive kiosk, video game, flash animation or menu based presentation opens up a world of branching choices for the developer. Each choice represents two or more possible directions the story or experience will take. For the script writer, these branches all have to be created on the page before they can be produced. One approach to getting to the heart of these branches is to create a flow chart at the head of the script. This flow chart defines each user choice, including those that loop back to a previous state, and helps to setup a method of enumerating these choices for the development team.

Anyone who has cracked a book or taken a class about screenwriting knows that there are "format purists" that demand absolute adherence to a set of screenplay formatting guidelines. These may vary, but at least in the case of the Hollywood screenplay there are some well-reasoned standards that help everyone understand what they are seeing when reading a screenplay. These formats are easily achieved by using a variety of excellent programs like the expensive Final Draft or the free online Celtix. These programs not only help to automatically format your script, but also help to manage frequently used character names, locations, etc. Plus, like any good word processor, these programs can help with spelling and grammar mistakes. Some even include alternate formats for two column layouts which are more common for commercials, or other productions that might feature narration.

It is important to understand the common rules for formatting, and to adhere to these when it seems appropriate; however, understanding that you can break these rules at will can be freeing when you are working on a challenging project. There have been many cases where the client's vision introduced challenges that helped me and my team to create new layouts, combine different styles, or simply wing it in a way that best helped the flow of production. Many of the examples in this book would make the "format purists" cringe. Some were simply thrown together quickly based on the timeframe of the project and thus lack a polished layout, and others started from atypical source material like Power Point slides or a marketing pdf and then were built around those. Others may start with a table of contents or flow chart and then break into individual modules, mixing Hollywood style, with 2 or 3 column layouts. In all cases that story backbone or the project blueprint was the goal. The script was always created to best communicate to the team the vision that the client had agreed to.

Scripts go through many drafts. Once the client has given their final sign-off and production is ready to go, it is often the case that the script goes through even more change. Many times a final draft of a script which seems tight, to the point, and concise, produces a first cut that feels extremely long, slow paced, and boring. This is where the script gets its true final draft in the cutting room, as redundant points are chopped or entire scenes are eliminated.

As a director I've had to cut some of my favorite scenes from a project, scenes that took maybe hundreds of hours of combined work to complete, because in the end, they did not move the story forward or said something that was better said in a different section of the production. The point here is that the script is a working, living document. Even with weeks of hard work, client input, and many revisions, the script is still a blueprint and not the final product. Of the examples in this book, I would bet there isn't a single one where the final product is a word for word match to what was on the final draft.

Screenwriting isn't rocket science (unless you include the script that is actually about rocket science later in this book). It's also not easy. Writing for the corporate world requires a basic understanding of that world. It requires thoughtful consultation with the client to not only come up with a story or a gimmick, but to understand who the audience for the production will be, how they will see it, and what it is you want them to do afterward. While working with the client or sometimes a team of clients, the writer and producer must solicit their creativity and knowledge. The client is not only paying for your work, they are also putting their reputation on the line, knowing that they will be represented by the final product, whether its purpose it is to sell a new gadget, train new employees, brag to their superiors, beg for department money, or to show the community how great their business is. Media production is as much about ego as it is about its stated purpose. It is about the ego of the client who brings the need and the money. It's about the egos of those actors or interviewees that appear onscreen, and it's about the ego of you and the creative team. Everyone has a stake in the final outcome, and working with the client is the first step in exploring that dynamic and putting those egos to work.

I've found that the best clients are wannabe producers themselves. Some have been involved with enough productions that they actually had more experience than I did, but were simply too busy to manage another task. Others were film enthusiasts and were assigned the responsibility to shepherd the project. In every case, the client knew more about the subject matter than me. They were the Subject Matter Expert or "SME".

"SME" became an important term for me as a producer and as a writer. When working on a production our team tried to identify one SME on the client side, anointing them as the go-to person. We also tried, often in our contract, to make them the ONLY go to person for anything that required a decision. The SME was responsible for getting us approved marketing points. They were the sole signer on script approval, and ultimately they were the one to approve the final product. This arrangement became critical, because the in the layered nature of digital media production, one small change near the end of the schedule can cause chaos. Something as simple as changing a line of narration requires rescheduling narration talent, booking studio time, re-editing a sequence, remixing the audio and re-mastering the final piece. Something as huge as replacing a cast member is even more catastrophic – a lesson we learned early on during a large production. With the proper understanding and a constant flow of communication with the SME, these problems can be minimized and when they do pop up, then change orders with proper budget adjustments can be made to correct the problem.

Having a good relationship with the SME can benefit to a production in many ways. In brainstorming, the SME can help come up with the best approach to achieve their goals. Their understanding of the subject and audience will help the team create something fresh and fun to create. As was our inclination, we often would allow the craziest ideas to emerge in early meetings with the SME. Always looking to emerging technologies, we pushed the creative process to find exciting new ways to tell the client's story, and the SME was usually right there coming up with some of the best stuff. Equally importantly, they were having a blast while doing it – a nice perk to a sometimes mundane job. Some of our brainstorming sessions led to videos that were constructed to play over six monitors at once, one project that was shot and shown entirely in a vertical orientation, an immersive 3D video that played in an Imax-like tradeshow dome, and many futuristic kiosk installations. We even made a video that ended with a digital cue that rotated a theater screen into the wall, leading the audience into an interactive space through the opening. All of these projects were co-created with the client. The scripts for these projects were offshoots of spirited brainstorming sessions.

In the examples of this book I will try to give a context to each project. Much of this is from memory, but there are also some additional production documents that will shed some light on the production process. Hopefully the scripts will show how one little spark from a brainstorming session became the hook that the entire project was based around. Maybe it is my particular taste, but I think the weirder the idea, the better. Some of these ideas were out in left field when we plucked them and built them into a final production. One idea that I regret we never got a chance to make was based around a funhouse ride. We were pitching to Cisco to create an experiential Customer Briefing Center and we proposed that a visiting group would board a line of Funhouse cars and take a ride through an interactive world of media and Cisco products. It would have been amazing. Maybe someday.

The production process is just that – a process. Changes are part of the mix at every stage of a production, and the scripts here are evidence of this. In each case I tried to find the final production script for each project. As you'll discover, the scripts are not always complete and in some cases, entire scenes that appear in the script were produced, edited and the yanked from the final projects. This was the result of many factors including the challenges of length, client preferences, technical gremlins and other factors. A few of the scripts contain the act of a change in mid process. Rather than trying to clean these up, I've decided to leave them exactly as they were. If you get the chance to view the final videos created from these scripts, I'm hoping you'll get a sense of how things improve over time. Often what seemed clear on the page was tweaked during the shoot, edit, sound sessions, and during several rounds of client reviews to land on the final produced versions. When I had gained enough experience to embrace this ever evolving process, I think I became a much better producer and writer.

Chapter 3: Conglomo and CTI
Marketing, Hollywood Style

Most of the early video pieces we produced at VisionFactory were animation heavy reinterpretations of marketing bullet points. They contained flashy graphics and kinetic text meant to bring the words from marketing one sheets to life. Often these were embedded in interactive CD-ROM projects as part of a larger package. In this sense, the video department served a support function to the interactive department. We kept hoping a project would come along that would allow us to branch out into storytelling and make a more narrative piece. Having just finished work on my first feature film, I was excited when a project called CTI came along. It was our chance to write a screenplay with multiple characters, dialog and several shooting locations. I loved the idea of continuity editing and creating a well-paced story in the style of a short film. We knew the challenges that a project like this would bring, but we also knew the client would be excited to come along for the ride.

CTI stood for Computer Telephony Integration. In layman's terms this meant combining a phone system with a computer interface and software to provide many more features to the end user. Nortel's Norstar phone system was already a digital phone controller that allowed a small business to manage several lines, navigate through a voicemail system and handle things like call forwarding, conference calls, and other features. The idea of CTI opened up a vast range of new features like communicating with a user database, retrieving customer information, storing call data and much more. CTI bridged the analog world with the digital world in a way that could be leveraged for more productivity by a wide range of small businesses.

When approached by the Norstar marketing team, we pitched a way of telling multiple small business stories within the context of a corporate boardroom meeting. The pitch went like this: The CEO of our fictional company Conglomo is not pleased about the company's lack of competitiveness and introduces a consultant that goes around the table one by one to the division heads to explain how CTI can help them to streamline operations and bring up their performance. This branches off into individual vignettes that demonstrate the CTI features in action, always returning to the board room for a little wrap up before going on to the next division.

The script approach was written both as a way to cohesively present several examples within a larger storyline and to allow our shooting schedule with several actors to remain to a maximum of two days. We knew the boardroom shoot would be the most logistically challenging and expensive, so we decided to knock it out as quickly as possible. Another plus from this script structure is the concept I return to frequently when discussing writing for marketing – modularity. The individual vignettes of the piece each represent a stand-alone idea or mini narrative that could be repurposed as part of an interactive piece. This concept of modularity was a big selling point for all of the content we began creating for Nortel. We were already envisioning a time when these modules might become part of a larger library of marketing collateral. Eventually we began referring to modules such as these as "Packets", borrowing the term from internet technology.

Writing the script for the CTI video was a throw-back to a couple of years earlier when I co-wrote my feature film Immortal. Creating these characters and developing a story flow allowed the creative freedom to throw some humor into the script while the marketing wish list provided the required actions that had to be woven in. The idea of people around a table telling a story may have seemed as original as a cheap porn script, but it did create a structure that built upon itself and led to a logical flow. There was an all-important beginning, middle, and end, and the product demonstrations served a purpose of moving the story along. Plus, the characters enabled a comical back and forth.

The one problem however was the amount of story we tried to tell. We tried to cram too many vignettes into a single linear piece. As pleased as I was at the time with the piece we created, I know now that is was much too long to hold an audience. That lesson was a great one to learn early in my career at VisionFactory. The audience will start going bleary-eyed after about seven minutes. I don't know why that's the number, but it constituently comes up. Over seven minutes and you'd better have something really exciting in there. Maybe that's why all of the Warner Brothers cartoons wrap things up around seven minutes. Anyway, the CTI piece was a wonderful experiment in Hollywood style marketing. The piece allowed us to create a mini movie and still work in some animation and flat out marketing. For the production team it helped us to grow immensely and set our sights on even more ambitious projects.

Included here are some support documents from the productions and a copy of a late version of the script. Particularly interesting is the CTI Video Production Heuristic which was created by my boss at the time Michael Worthington. The flow chart was one device that allowed us to wrap our heads around the project and all of the dependent elements that had to be created and coordinated.

The CTI project introduced one final lesson – the importance of casting. Originally we had cast a young actor and writer who had just starred in his first feature film to play the lead role of Frank Johnson. Johnson addressed the boardroom group for much of the film and was written as a sort of narrator device. The actor was in his mid-twenties and had an all American military look. The client signed off on the casting choices and we went into full production with this actor. It wasn't until after we had completed a fine cut of the video that the client came back and decided that they weren't happy with the performance. It had a harsh edge to it and they wanted to go in a different direction.

Reluctantly, we called in some other actors, finally selecting a fellow film-school student I had worked with years before. He had a much more pleasant delivery, softening the criticism delivered in the script. This choice meant reshooting the boardroom scenes which we were able to do in a single day. This also meant recalling all of the actors, crew, wardrobe, and gear. It was an expensive lesson. But in the end the client was thrilled with the results.

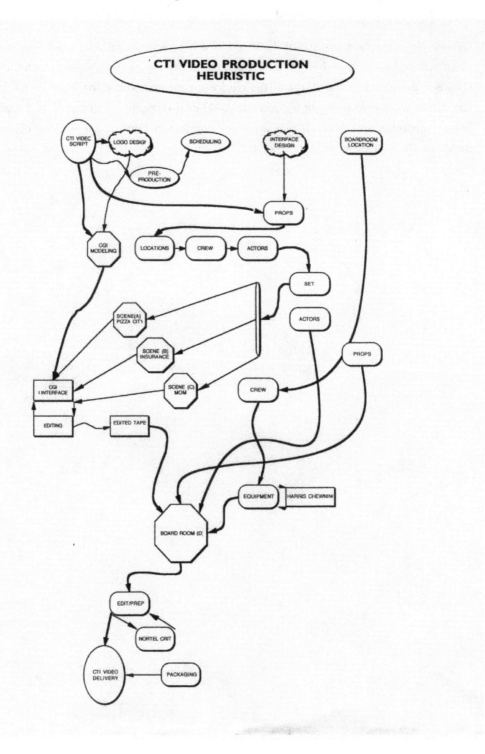

Figure 3-1: This serpentine creation mapped the process of producing the CTI project.

Figure 3-2: The fictional corporation Conglomo featured an impressive spinning 3D logo animated by Eric Jones that opened the video.

Characters:

C.E.O. a middle aged man with graying hair

FRANK JOHNSON a young white male who has an air of "College Business Nerd" about him, number crunching head of facilities and operations for Conglomo

PHILIP MORGAN a distinguished looking older white male, V.P. and head of Semiconductor Warehouse

BRITTA ROBERTS a black woman in her thirties, V.P. and head of PIZZA CITY

CATHERINE FRYE oriental female in her thirties. C.C.Insurance Agency V.P.

DELORES PACKARD a middle aged female V.P. of Conglomo Corp. customer service

MAXWELL SWIFT young white male. Stylish, trendy and V.P. of Statement fashions

CONGLOMO and CTI

Third Draft
December 4, 1996
Writer: Steve White

FADE IN:

EXT. CONGLOMO CORPORATE HEADQUARTERS - DAY

The building is a large ominous structure, very Art Deco in
Design. It speaks of a huge corporation. This is perhaps a
virtual 3d rendering. The camera cranes down from a high point in
the sky to ground level and the CONGLOMO Sign fills the
foreground. It is in the shape of the earth with the words
"CONGLOMO CORP." spinning around it a'la Universal Pictures.

Music here accentuates the mood, dark, ominous. A voice mixes up
while we're still on the exterior shot. It is distant.

                         C.E.O.
               Ladies and Gentlemen of the board, we are
               falling behind. We are at a crossroads
               for the Conglomo Corporation, and frankly
               I can't explain how we got here.

As the distant voice grows louder and closer, the exterior image
dissolves to:

INT. CONFERENCE ROOM - DAY

A CRANE DOWN from the ceiling of a large boardroom reveals a large
conference table that is lined with executives all focusing
forward on the speaker, a middle aged man with graying hair, the
C.E.O. Though it is light outside, there is no sign of that here.
The room is dark sparing the pools of light on the C.E.O., and on
the Vice Presidents that surround the large table, and on several
large posters that hang on the room's perimeter (see production
notes about posters).

                         C.E.O
                    (continuing)
               We have gone from the industry leader in
               many of our divisions, to second, third
               and even fourth in some of our markets.

The camera pans the rows of V.P.s on either side of the table.
This is an interesting mix of people. Included are Frank Johnson,
a young white male who has an air of "College Business Nerd" about
him, Britta Roberts, a black woman in her thirties, Delores
Packard, middle-aged, Philip Morgan- somewhat rough looking
fiftyish union boss type, Catherine Frye oriental in her thirties
and Maxwell Swift, a stylish trendy fashion plate in his late
twenties. It is a cross-section of the CONGLOMO work force which
has divisions all over the world. Behind each of these V.P's is a
poster for the division of CONGLOMO which they head.

                         C.E.O.
                    (continuing)
               Now, the reason we've called this meeting
               is twofold. First - we've got to

NORSTAR/CTI VIDEO - THIRD DRAFT DEC 4, 1996
Confidential: Not For Disclosure Without The Permission
of Information Design Corporation

determine how we got here, and second - we
must act to reverse this trend.

The faces of the V.P.'s look worried. They know they've fallen
behind. The faces lighten somewhat as the C.E.O. continues.

                              C.E.O.
                    (continuing)
          Now we're not here to assign blame, at
          least not yet. We're looking for
          solutions.

The C.E.O. looks to the young man at the table.

                              C.E.O.
          Johnson.

Johnson, in his mid twenties, looking right out of college steps
up to the front of the table as the C.E.O. takes a seat to the
side. Johnson wears wire framed glasses and holds a remote
control in his hand. He directs the control to the back of the
room and presses a button. Behind Johnson is a movie screen.

                              JOHNSON
          We have uncovered an alarming trend among
          our small business competitors that
          explains much about our market share loss.
          Through creative applications of Computer
          Telephony Integration, more commonly known
          as C.T.I., small businesses are able to
          reduce overhead, improve service and
          increase productivity. Our competitors
          are beating us by using technology more
          effectively than we are.

As he speaks a video projector that rests at the back end of the
table fires up. The beam from the lens throws an elaborate image
on the screen. The image is sectioned off into blocks of text and
graphics, with one window which is for video playback. In the
upper Left corner is a computer animation of the Conglomo logo.
Other blocks feature scrolling and crawling text, as well as a
window of graphics flashing and changing,   each new picture is a
logo for one of Conglomo's many divisions. THE SCREEN IS
ASSEMBLED IN A FUNCTIONAL FASHION "THE FUTURE LOOK OF WINDOWS"

As Johnson speaks of C.T.I. the words "Computer Telephony
Integration appear on the screen as well as the initials CTI in a
larger font. The video window displays a montage of images
related to CTI including still images of Hardware, computer
screens in action, people using CTI applications at their desktops
and on location. (these are snippets from the vignettes that will
be shown).

An arm goes up at the table. It is that of Philip, head of
Semiconductor Warehouse.

                              PHILIP

I'm afraid you've already lost me. What
is this Computer Tele-phoney and how can
it make such a dramatic difference?

                    JOHNSON
          Well, Computer Telephony, let's just use
          C.T.I. C.T.I. on the most basic level is
          the marriage of your telephone system with
          your computer. This allows the user to
          direct and route calls, as well as
          integrate the customer database and other
          computer information with the telephone
          system.

The graphic display behind him changes as Johnson explains the
basics of C.T.I.

                    JOHNSON
               (continuing)
          By using custom software, the user can
          turn their phone system into an
          intelligent routing system and trigger
          computer applications by incoming phone
          calls.

                    PHILIP
          This is still sort of a mystery to me
          Frank. How does this CTI benefit a small
          business?

Others around the table nod in agreement with the question. Faces
show confusion.

                    JOHNSON
          That's what I hope to show you tonight.
          Let's look at some examples. Britta,
          what is PIZZA CITY's biggest expense?

Britta, seated before the large PIZZA CITY banner turns to reply.

                    BRITTA
          Well, in most markets it's payroll.

                    JOHNSON
          And if you could reduce payroll costs
          that would translate to more profit.

                    BRITTA
          That's true, but I don't want to
          jeopardize customer service.

Johnson presses a button on his remote which expands and brings to
the foreground and a map of North America on the screen behind
him. It is an active weather map as well as a detailed "dot" map
of Conglomo business locations.

                    JOHNSON

We've conducted some surveillance missions
in certain markets, and I think you'll be
interested in what we uncovered.

The Video begins to roll within the window on the screen. It
expands to fill the screen once the image appears then, on cue the
map zooms into .....

                         JOHNSON
              Scottsdale Arizona.

The red dot that is Scottsdale pops to fill the map window. The
Video window replaces it. Beside this window is the "method"
window showing the surveillance technique used to recover the
footage. In the "method window is a pair of eyeglasses, rotating
as if on a product platter. A text and pointer describe the
camera that is hidden in the frame. (this window is eyecandy, and
doesn't necessarily have to be on long enough to get the whole
meaning.)

                                                    CUT TO:

(Full screen of the video presentation.)

EXT. CAPITOL CREATIONS PIZZA - DAY

Smooth traveling shot glides down a city street as a row of shops
pass through the frame. The front of a Pizza Parlor comes into
view as the camera ramps down to a static shot. The camera zooms
in on the window, we can see activity inside. Johnson narrates
the scene for the group around the table.

                         JOHNSON (O.S.)
              This is PIZZA CITY's number one competitor
              in Scottsdale, a little mom-and-pop owned
              parlor. For 10 years we've owned this
              market, but last year something changed.

POV of Surveillance camera, eye level. He walks toward and then
into the Pizza parlor.

INT. PIZZA PARLOR - DAY

Surviellance cam POV. Behind the counter a young lady addresses
Steve (directly to the lens).

                         LADY
              Can I help you?

                         STEVE (O.S.)
              I'll have a large pepperoni to go please.

The camera wanders the room and settles on a computer terminal
behind the counter. The phones rings. The camera holds on the
terminal as the girl at the counter walks over to the terminal.

As the phone rings a series of things happen on the terminal screen.

These include:

A row of buttons pop up at the bottom of the screen.
A window pops up with the information of the caller's name, address, last five orders and special instruction and directions to his house appear.

These are all features of Visit Fastcall.

The girl answers the phone call by touching the screen of her computer. She speaks into the monitor, the PC is equipped with a speakerphone.

                         LADY
              Capitol Creations, may I help you.

                    CUSTOMER VOICE
              Yes, I'd like to order a large crispy
              deluxe.

The lady traces her finger along the information window on the screen as she talks to the customer. (see window information design.)

                         LADY
              OK. Mr. Spear,   that's with no olives
              correct?

                       CUSTOMER
              That's right.

                         LADY
              And you need this delivered to 2100 Spring
              St.?

                       CUSTOMER
              That's right!

                         LADY
              Great. Your total will be $14.63 and
              we'll be there in about 25 minutes.

                       CUSTOMER
              Wonderful. Thanks very much.

                         LADY
              Thank you Mr. Spear.

There is a laser printer on the counter. It is spitting out as sheet of paper that includes all the information pertaining to the order including:
The Pizza details, the price and total, persons name, the directions to the home with a graphical map, telephone number, and even coupons on the bottom of the page. (diagram)

The girl takes the sheet from the printer, tapes it to a pizza box and slides it back to the cook.

CUT TO:

INT. CONFERENCE ROOM

Close on Britta as she looks toward the screen. She has a look of "wow" about her. Johnson presses his remote and the video in the window freezes on the image of the Pizza box with the paper taped to it.

                    JOHNSON
          Let's look at this closely. The parlor is
          using an application called Visit Fastcall
          developed by Nortel.

The "Data" window in the multi-media presentation goes full screen. It shows the image from the computer monitor used by the girl at the pizza place. The image changes as Johnson describes what happens.

                    JOHNSON
          When the phone rings, the computer
          automatically reads the caller ID
          information, pops up a row of choices and
          calls up the specific customer's file from
          the database.

The screen shows a close up of the Database information.

                    JOHNSON
                  (continuing)
          The database in this case shows the
          customer's name, address and phone number,
          as well as the five orders, arming the
          clerk with a wealth of information about
          the customer before even answering the
          call. The entire order takes about 16
          seconds.

Wide now on Johnson. He picks up a piece of paper and holds it up.

                    JOHNSON
                  (continuing)
          The computer prints out a combination
          receipt, delivery map, ... and even
          coupons.

Johnson hands the paper to someone at the table to pass to Britta.

                    JOHNSON
          This restaurant was able to dramatically
          reduce payroll overhead, streamline its
          order taking and deliveries, and form a
          better bond with the customer all because
          of this simple C.T.I. application.

Britta looks up to Johnson.

                    BRITTA
          What about the database, if we used a
          system like this would we have to replace
          our existing customer database software?

                    JOHNSON
          No, the application is designed to support
          any computer application, and is very easy
          to configure. In answer to your question,
          even our proprietary software can easily
          be integrated with Fastcall.

CATHERINE FRYE oriental male in his forties and C.C.Insurance
Agency V.P. addresses Johnson.

                    CATHERINE
          I see your point about a Pizza Parlor, but
          how can C.T.I. help the rest of us?

                    JOHNSON
          Well Catherine, let's look at the
          Insurance business. how much time do your
          agents spend using the telephone?

                    CATHERINE
          I'm not really sure. Probably 30 to 40%
          of their day is spent communicating on the
          phone. It's our biggest sales tool.

                    JOHNSON
          Exactly. It's the most common way they
          communicate with the client.

                    CATHERINE
          But honestly, it's often very frustrating
          for our agents and clients when a call is
          improperly forwarded, or gets lost in
          voice mail.

Johnson presses his remote control bringing the map again to the
foreground then zooming into....

                    JOHNSON
          Edmonton, Alberta. This is the regional
          office of Sunshine Insurance.

A video starts in the window. It shows the exterior of an office
building. In the "Method" window are two security camera models.
One is pivoting and tilting on its base. The words "Intercepted
Video" appear below the graphic. Once again this method window is
only up for a moment.

Johnson stands before the screen while the video plays.

                    JOHNSON

> Once again our surveillance team conducted
> a mission to determine why this upstart
> company was able to dramatically cut our
> market share in the region.

The video image goes full screen as we CUT TO:

Black and White video image, static noise fills the screen and
clears to reveal:

INT. OFFICES OF SUNSHINE INSURANCE -DAY

A high angle shot, down on the lobby of the Sunshine Insurance
offices.

                    JOHNSON (o.s.)
          Our boys were able to intercept the
          security camera signals from within the
          structure allowing us to observe the day
          to day activity here.

The images are cutting from one security camera angle to another.
Each is a high angle, Black and white. There is a rhythm to the
cuts, nothing spectacular is happening within the shots. Several
folks talking on the phone. The receptionist greeting folks in
the lobby. One camera (maybe all) zooms, pans and tilts in a
jerking fashion, like a remote controlled security cam would have-
very mechanical.

                    JOHNSON
          After many uneventful days we started to
          notice a surprising pattern. It seems
          that every time the phone rang it
          automatically was directed to the agent or
          staffer the person wanted to speak to. We
          know there are only a couple of phone
          lines going into those offices, but it
          consistently happened as if the phone
          system knew who the caller wanted to talk
          to.

CUT TO:

INT. CONFERENCE ROOM

Catherine is watching the front of the room. Johnson looks to the
screen.

                    JOHNSON
          Here we've reconstructed what was
          happening with these phone calls.

This description is accompanied by an elaborate animation sequence
that shows an overhead view of the office complex floor plan and
has glowing lines representing the phonelines within the walls and
leading into the phone set. This layout is common for a Norstar

system interfaced with individual? PC's throughout the office
complex.   (logistics here??)

                        JOHNSON
                    (continuing)
            A client's call comes in here into a
            Norstar phone system. The system
            communicates the incoming caller's phone
            number to this PC, and the call is
            automatically routed to the agent that
            handles that client. An if the agent is
            out, or on the line then the call can be
            routed to the agent's voice-mail, or to
            another agent.

Wide shot on the table over Johnson's shoulder. Catherine
interjects:

                        CATHERINE
            How does it work?

                        JOHNSON
            This is another powerful feature of Visit
            Fastcall- the ability to route calls based
            on simple sets of instructions defined by
            the user.

*Details here accompanied by screen shots of programming
preferences in visit fastcall (using the demo).*

Preferences also show the call database, timer, ...

Detailed???Specifics on Nortel products????

                        DELORES
            What about installation of this system?
            Is that the big catch?

                        JOHNSON
            We suspected that a system this powerful
            and flexible must be very complex so we
            had our top engineers look into how
            difficult installation is.

Johnson looks to the screen, presses his remote. The video window
shows a doorway. Into the frame walks two then three men in white
engineer lab coats, they open the door and walk through
motivating the camera to follow at a distance into:

INT. LARGE WAREHOUSE SPACE - DAY

The room is huge and empty except for a table in the center with
three items on it, a PC, a Norstar system?? and a teleadapter
TAD device. This looks like a shot out of THX, stark room, the
space in the room just makes what is on the table seem more
important.

                        JOHNSON
            Here is what is at the heart of the system
            the _____ also know as a TAD or _____.
            Here our top engineer connects the Tad to
            the PC and another engineer attaches the
            _____ connector to the Norstar phone
            system.

This transpires onscreen. The simplicity is presented almost in
hyperbole. This drives home the point "this is really easy to
do."

BOARDROOM

The faces around the table look to the screen anticipating more.
Pregnant pause here.

                        MAXWELL
            What else?

                        JOHNSON
            That's it.

Around the table the faces are impressed. A couple of the folks
take notes.

The C.E.O. perks up. His look is inquisitive.

                        C.E.O.
            Delores, haven't you used this C.T.I.
            technology within your call centers for a
            few years now?

                        DELORES

Well, yes we have used similar technology
to manage customer calls and to build our
sales and warrantee databases. But I had
no idea this technology was available on
the franchise level.

                    JOHNSON
        It's true that CTI has been in use by
        major call centers, service lines etc. for
        many years now. It just makes sense to
        use computers to manage 200-300 phones and
        we've been very successful with that. But
        now we're seeing the same powerful
        technology applied by companies with one
        or two phone lines.

The setup here is for either Permanent Records, or the Fashion
store that challenges Statement. If Permanent records then
exploit the use of the web to collect customer files and interests
and have the CTI Application communicate with the caller ID
function to serve the customer a customized list of choices.
Voice response, customized voice mail, navigate through audio
samples --24hours a day.

Johnson once again presses his remote.   On screen the map in the
video window now goes toward North Carolina.

                    JOHNSON
        R.T.P., North Carolina. This is the home
        of Permanent Records, a small business
        distributor of cassettes and CD's that has
        become a serious competitor to Conglomo's
        own "DIALTUNES" .

                                              CUT TO:

EXT. PERMANENT RECORDS - DAY

A door opens at the front of the building. Ben, mid twenties,
pokes his head out and looks directly at the camera in the
distance. He pokes his head back into the building and in a
moment returns with another man, Paul and they both look toward
the camera, then begin walking toward it.

                    JOHNSON
        The owners spotted our surveillance team
        and actually asked them in for coffee.

The image goes black for a moment and then returns now as:

INT. PERMANENT RECORDS - DAY

Close up on a coffee table as a cup of coffee is served up. A
series of cuts are involved in this video since the team actually
can move around within the space. It is a more traditionally cut
sequence.

                              JOHNSON
                   Ben and Paul, the owners were very happy
                   to show us the streamlined sales system
                   they had developed.

Ben sits before a computer terminal and demonstrates how Permanent
uses their website to build an international database of
customers, detailing phone info, address, musical interests and
taking preliminary orders. They then use CTI to integrate the
database with incoming callers and to prompt a suggestion list of
similar music. They also use visit Voice to manage an interactive
voice mail system that allows callers to listen to short clips
from CDs and to request a fax back service of the latest
catalogue.

The Fashion Bug Direct --a chance to create a really nice
teleconferencing setup where the distributor in the US
communicates with colleges in Milan and Paris via a video
conferencing interface.

Delores faces Johnson.

                              DELORES
                   Just how expensive is this technology?

                              JOHNSON
                   It is surprisingly affordable, with basic
                   systems starting under $1000. (????) And
                   since the system can be seamlessly
                   integrated with the already existing PC or
                   Mac in the office environment, it's an
                   upgrade that adds value, increases
                   productivity and just makes sense.

                              DELORES
                   So we could upgrade our systems without
                   that big of an investment.

                              JOHNSON
                   Exactly. Many of the components are
                   already in place.

                              PHILIP

OK. What about my warehouse guys? We've
invested in the Companion wireless system
for the whole site. Now we don't have
computers on the fork-lifts. What good is
this C.T.I. to me?

                    JOHNSON
          It's a good question. One concern we've
          had at corporate is how does C.T.I. fit
          into products we've already invested in?

Johnson presses his remote and another clip begins playing. The
clip goes full screen.

CUT TO:

EXT. LARGE WAREHOUSE PARKING LOT - DAY

                    JOHNSON (O.S.)
          This is CHIPS AHOY, our largest competitor
          in the semiconductor market.

The image cuts to a traveling shot from the "hidden camera." The
shots within the warehouse have a nice gliding quality to them -
motivated by the fact they are shot from the fork-lift.

                    JOHNSON
               (continuing)
          This facility uses the same Companion
          system that we have installed in all of
          our warehouses. Only we found some
          interesting new twists.

The camera dollies in and focuses on an employee who stands beside
a large row of shelves. Stacks of cardboard boxes, all alike,
line the shelves. He talks into his Companion handset, then pulls
it from his ear to view the LCD readout.

-----LOGISTICS NEEDED HERE: WHAT DOES THE INTERACTION WITH AN
INVENTORY DATABASE LOOK LIKE WITH THE COMPANION SET?? IS THIS
FEASIBLE?-----
(The example is to show a wireless interaction w/the inventory
database while the worker is still able to communicate with the
customer. What are the best products to exploit here? What about
the thing from the trade show that you wear around your neck?)

                    JOHNSON
          Here the warehouse worker is able to
          access his inventory and physically verify
          that a product is ready to ship, letting
          the customer know on the spot. Also, if a
          part is out of stock, he can immediately
          place an order or search for a substitute
          without running back to the office.

The camera moves with the worker as he walks to another group of shelves.

                    JOHNSON
          The Companion system dramatically
          increased our productivity when we first
          installed it in our facilities, and now
          we have an opportunity to make it even
          more powerful.

THE BOARDROOM

Philip is impressed. Now he has that "wow" look about his generally conservative face. he glances at the table.

Close up on a small pad in front of him. Just below two scribbled games of tic-tac-toe he writes the initials - "C.T.I." We've won over Philip. Johnson still speaks during these shots.

                    JOHNSON
          This powerful, portable solution increased
          the warehouse efficiency while reducing
          the workload. More sales were made because
          the inventory was managed better.

Johnson looks to Philip.

                    JOHNSON
          So what do you think Philip?

                    PHILIP
          I think our boys could use something like
          that.

Johnson holds up the remote control he's been using. It is a Companion handset.

                    JOHNSON
          Here's another example of CTI. This is my
          Companion handset. With a few simple
          software commands, I've used CTI to make
          this my screen remote. The hotkeys simply
          emulate my old remote and I can actually
          talk to technicians, my boss, or order a
          pizza while doing a presentation. Right
          now I have the system set to forward my
          calls to voice mail, but with a couple of
          keys reset so calls come directly here.

Johnson clicks his remote and the screen displays a large animation of the letters "CTI".

                    JOHNSON
          So here we have a dilemma. As one of the
          world leaders in the use of technology in
          business are falling behind the our
          competitors who are constantly inventing

new ways to use C.T.I. Let's just take a
look at these few examples again.

Johnson clicks his remote again starting the recap video.

                    JOHNSON
          We've seen examples of simple uses of CTI
          to expedite an order, streamline
          production cut delivery time.

On screen are shots of Lady taking the pizza order, flip
transition to taping the laser printed paper to the pizza box,
flip transition to close up tilt down of the sheet showing the
detailed map to the customer's house.

                    JOHNSON
          We've also seen C.T.I. applied to
          intelligently route calls and to manage
          voice mail and conference calls .

Images from the insurance sequence are recapped here.

                    JOHNSON
          An ingenious combination of the Companion
          handset and an inventory database showed
          us how C.T.I. can go portable, and how we
          can integrate some of the superior
          products we already use with this new
          technology.

Images from the warehouse here.

                    JOHNSON
          And we saw another company that built
          their entire sales technique around the
          benefits of C.T.I. by combining the web,
          their customer and inventory databases,
          voice mail management and an automated
          ordering system.

Images here from Permanent Records.

                    JOHNSON
          The amazing thing about C.T.I. is that
          we've only scratched the surface with
          these examples, and many of the uses of
          CTI within Conglomo haven't even been
          imagined yet. With over 20000?? software
          developers producing solutions for the CTI
          marketplace, and with the Nortel hardware
          we already use, I can see Conglomo
          pioneering new applications of CTI to
          better manage our communication needs, and
          increase productivity and profit
          throughout the Conglomo family.

We all know that communication is the key
to business success, and up to now I
thought we were doing a pretty good job.
But it's a new world out there. We can
either take advantage of these
opportunities involving C.T.I., or watch
the little guy who does move into our
corner offices while we're moving out.

Johnson looks to the C.E.O. who stares up and down the table. The
camera scans the faces of the V.P.'s stopping on a Close up of the
CEO.

                    C.E.O.
               There's just one thing I want to know.
               Why haven't we already been taking
               advantage of this technology?

There is an uncomfortable silence about the room. The C.E.O.
looks to Johnson.

                    JOHNSON
               Well, frankly sir, nobody thought of it.

The camera pulls back from the Close shot of Johnson as the
meeting is ending. It glides back and up into the ceiling and
passes by the spinning globe with the Conglomo logo circling.

FADE OUT.

Tag onto end "The future of C.T.I."

This is a quick treatment of a proposed ending for the video that
addresses the future of CTI and also suggests the path that the
CEO of Conglomo takes for the company.

After fading to black a title is spurred. It reads "In the not
so distant future..."

Once again we are on the exterior of the Conglomo Corp.
headquarters. It is dusk as the CEO walks to his car. He enters
and presses a button on the dash which "calls" his secretary.

Inside the Conglomo complex, seated behind a modern streamlined
desktop is the secretary. She wears an ultra light headset
(doesn't even look like a headset). Before her what resembles a
sheet of Plexiglas angled upright on her desk. It has about the
same surface space as a standard computer monitor. A tone rings
out softly.

"Yes Mr. Peterson," she responds as the Plexiglas fades up the image of the CEO seated inside of his car. "Any messages" he asks and she reads a few. Then small talk begins.

"What are your weekend plans?" she asks. As he describes going home and relaxing with a nice cup of tea, a barbecue roast, and a soak in the hot tub, a series of shots happen.

First there is a reaction on a computer-like interface at the CEO's home. a tone rings and activity begins on the screen. As he lists the things he is planning to do, each spoken item sets into motion an activity. For instance, when he mentions the hot tub, a valve opens, beginning to fill the hot tub and to heat the water. The roast is set to bake in a high tech microwave and so on.

This is a quick sketch of a really ambitious look at the future of CTI. Some of this may be beyond the scope of this project. I realize the future of CTI will look more and more like the "Jetsons."

Chapter 4: Internet Thruway

The lesson of the glowing rice

The early days of VisionFactory involved times of feast and famine. Like any start-up, we went through long periods without booking significant work. Then an occasional job would come in that consumed all of our resources around the clock. Corporate production seems to always come with an impossible deadline. When paying work was slow, we turned to internal marketing – keeping the production machine running and experimenting with new techniques. Fortunately, our team thrived on learning new things and being the first to achieve some breakthrough in interactive media.

We wisely began to network our offices and experiment with a connected workflow. The internet was still in its infancy and I can remember during my first days editing with the company, my day began around 6:00am logging onto America Online via a dialup modem to check my email. At least in that aspect, these were dark times. On many occasions we relied on what we called "sneaker net" to share files between developers. This entailed dumping a file to a disk and running it down the hall to another developer to pop it into their machine.

Our departments included video, interactive presentation programming, and design, though all disciplines overlapped somewhat. Developing CD-ROM based training pieces for our small stable of clients helped us to combine video and interactivity in new ways, and each project began to lead to even more opportunities. We grew quickly and soon took on more and more complex projects. One of these was a video for Nortel called "Internet Thruway" which was based on a product aimed at the telephone companies, to allow them to provide modem service directly to their clients.

Essentially, the home internet market up to that point was made up of enterprising local startups with a room full of modems attached to several landlines. These were the first ISPs. They were signing up subscribers, providing tech support, buying internet backbone through ISDN or T1 lines and sharing that connection via an often primitive array of modems, dependent upon a free landline being available for the customer. Anyone who remembers this time of dialup internet and local ISPs, also remembers the annoyance of trying to get through without a busy signal. And then of course the 14.4, 28.8, or 56k if you were lucky, analog modem speeds were just fast enough to deliver an image on a web page over the course of several seconds.

Internet Thruway was Nortel's solution to this market – an easy way for the telephone company to add banks of modems directly at the switch and start to gobble up these new customers. It was the local ISP killer, and Nortel needed a unique way to market it to the hundreds of telephone companies that were potential customers.

For the team at VisionFactory, Internet Thruway represented a nicely budgeted opportunity to try some new things. Our idea was to create a racing themed video that would combine 3D animation of a Formula One racecar with interviews of existing ISP owners and Nortel representatives. The racing sequences would show the new speeds that the equipment could achieve as well as illustrate other marketing points.

For the live interviews we were able to travel to a few cities including Minneapolis - St Paul, Dallas and Milwaukee. At each location we met with young entrepreneurs who had created a successful business providing internet connectivity. The headshot interviews with these business owners provided a sense of authenticity to the otherwise contrived video pieces. Those were slickly animated in LightWave 3D – with our main animator once again pushing the boundaries of computer processing power, memory, disk space and schedule. The results were down to the wire, but spectacular. For voice over talent we went with a local veteran who, though expensive, was the perfect match for the piece. The "voice of god" delivery was one we would rely on again and again in the coming years.

The video had a tight schedule since it was to be debuted as part of a trade show event. We had a drop dead date and it was a very close call in the end. The problem wasn't in getting all of the interviews in the can, but rather the ambitious animation sequences we had created for the piece. The race car metaphor pitted the Internet thruway car against slower alternatives. The script called for realistic looking 3d race cars and our animator took this seriously. He was already becoming an expert at the LightWave 3d software package and pushed the elements that he created to the maximum capabilities of the processor power and memory that our machines could handle. Once a sequence was locked, he would utilize the render farm he had created from every available PC on our network. Then came the waiting. Since this was still the mid 90's the machines weren't very powerful, and with one frame of animation taking up to 30 minutes to render, it was obvious we were going down to the wire. The script after all contained probably 4 solid minutes of animation.

As it became woefully obvious that LightWave couldn't possibly render all of the sections we needed in time, my boss shifted his strategy for a key sequence of the script. For overhead shots of the race, the blimp shots, we would create a sequence of what we termed the glowing rice. The 3d racetrack from above would feature heavily blurred graphics side by side on the track to represent the stages of the competition. If you imagine Mighty Mouse flying in the distance, with a glowing trail following behind, that was the look of our glowing rice cars. The pieces were done in After Effects, a 2D animation software package that required much less render time, while the more complex close-ups of the cars were being churned out frame by frame on the render farm. Surprisingly, when cut into the 3D pieces, it didn't look half bad.

The glowing rice saved our ass. We made our deadline with minutes to spare after a final 24 hour push. The resulting video had a wonderfully consistent metaphor, "wow" factor graphics, believable customer testimonials and professional narration. All of these factors resulted in a 7 minute video which helped establish VisionFactory as an exciting alternative to industry veterans competing for the same work.

Internet Thruway was an important piece for the company because it pushed us to our limits creatively and helped us to showcase our creativity to a large audience. The client used the piece in tradeshows, direct mailing and through the sales force. We used it to show other clients what we were capable of. The video won VisionFactory two ITVA awards that year, the first year we had entered anything. The video also led to a sequel called *Collaborate* which built upon the marketing points of the first video.

As it turned out, the Internet Thruway product offering was a first step toward other, more revolutionary products like the 1-Meg Modem which was essentially Nortel's first DSL equipment. Our success with the ambitious Internet Thruway video helped cement our relationship with a rapidly growing faction within Nortel, and VisionFactory was becoming known as a provider for top quality content for internet products. Since Nortel had built its decades old reputation by providing digital telephony switches for huge communications networks, it was in a prime position to compete in the worldwide market for the emerging internet backbone equipment. Our timing was purely accidental, but it was perfect to place VisionFactory as a key marketing partner for the company.

The script included in this chapter is for the second Internet Thruway video we created called *Collaborate*. The idea was to use a series of metaphors to illustrate the data networks and to illuminate ideas like limits in customer choice. With ideas like a child playing with tinker toys to show how complex the network was, or a restaurant where the only item on the menu was a hamburger, we took advantage of the script's freedom to explore new production techniques. This was the first time we used green screen to marry 3D animation with live action actors. It also allowed us to create the idea or quality and reliability through a beautifully animated sequence of a virtual music box. To my dismay, the completed sequence was ultimately cut by the client.

Through a little archeological work I recovered the script and some other production materials from this production including the original storyboards.

SCENE	AUDIO	VIDEO
		FADE IN
1.0	Intro Sequence	TITLE SUPER: "The Landscape"
	NARRATOR: It was a simple idea. Build a network to send voices across the land. We did it- and everything was good. Then modems started screeching across our voice network. It sounded like the mating calls of a European swallow – awful. And it just kept getting louder, and louder, and louder…	Extreme close-up of a small child's face (3-5 years old) lit by a single spotlight. He glances down. Child's POV of a tinker toy hub. His hand reaches for it. Series of close ups of the child's hands and eyes as he assembles tinker toys, making connections. The background and surrounding area falls off into black.
	EFX: The sound of modem handshaking takes over	A medium shot of the child begins a pull back through the structure that he has constructed before him, a large tinkertoy molecule. The continued pullback reveals an intricate network of tinker toys the size of a gymnasium.
	NARRATOR: ISPs loved it, carriers didn't mind either. But there had to be a better way to handle data traffic. The industry needed it, and Nortel made it happen with the worlds most successful Internet access solution – Internet Thruway.	Continuing this "virtual" dolly out through the structure of this massive network, the child is now far in the distance. The structure begins to glow as if electricity passes from connection to connection. As tinkertoy hubs pass from behind the camera and float into the distance some are mapped with video images. Images include: Shots of people using the internet. CO equipment, ISP equipment, business people using the net. The network is represented now by several hubs each representing a part of the voice/data network and emerging from the center of it all, is a glowing Internet Thruway emblem and Nortel logo. FADE OUT.

SCENE	AUDIO	VIDEO

2.0	The ISP "What's Going On?"
	
	NARRATOR:
	The landscape of the internet is changing rapidly for ISPs, Corporate WAN Administrators and Carriers. One day you think you've got it all figured out- and the next someone's telling you you've got no future. Those you thought were your enemies might now be allies. So who *do* you trust?
	
	ISP INTERVIEWEE: (need multiple voices)
	Addresses concerns:
	    Taking away terminating hardware (modems)
	    Competitive pressures from all directions
	    Identity as service provider without modems in the closet
	
	NARRATOR:
	What if you had the opportunity to shape the future of the internet? Not some rotating logo on a mail order, drink umbrella web site, but effect the entire future of data networking. Interested?
	
	ISP INTERVIEWEE:
	Addresses:
	
	NARRATOR:
	I think we have the start of a beautiful relationship.
		FADE IN
		
		TITLE SUPER: "What's Going On?"
		
		Two businessmen, ISP Sam and Carrier Ralph are seated at the table engrossed in a "tarot card" reading with a gypsy character. Each man has a portfolio resting in front of him. One has a graphic that reads "Carrier Projections", the other "ISP Growth" They hang on each turn of the cards.
		
		The first card in close-up. It is ornately decorated as tarot cards often are, with the image of a tinkertoy diagram with dollar signs in every hub.
		
		Both men grin-everybody wins.
		
		The next card shows the same graphic with the center hub missing. In its place is a dollar sign under a red circle with a line through it.
		
		The men-not happy about this- glance at one another then to the gypsy.
		
		Stylish "cinema verite" interview setups with pertinent interviewees (letterboxing on the interviews) and relevant B-roll.
		
		{possibly frame this bit through a crystal ball}
		Glib montage of shots of a rotating logo on a mail order drink umbrella web site (push off screen). Cut to shot of puzzled bubble gum chewing young programmer.
		
		The programmer looks up at the camera. Sure he's interested.
		
		Stylish "cinema verite" interview setups with pertinent interviewees (letterboxing on the interviews) and relevant B-roll
		
		Back at the tarot reading:
		Anticipation builds and the gypsy turns the final card to reveal an Internet Thruway logo and an image of two hands shaking.
		
		FADE OUT.

SCENE	AUDIO	VIDEO

3.0	The Carrier "See The Future"
	
	NARRATOR:
	Let's face it carriers - the voice network limits how you can handle data. You can send it from here to there, but what else?
	
	CARRIER INTERVIEWEE: (Need multiple voices)
	Addresses:
	   Limited data services
	   Unable to provide much to ISPs besides B channels
	   Need new revenue opportunities
	   Need to respond quicker to ISPs and Corp. WAN
	   (Enterprise) customers.
	
	NARRATOR:
	Hey, I have an idea. What if carriers and ISPs get together and create The New Internet? Internet Thruway can make it happen…
		FADE IN
		TITLE SUPER: "See The Future"
		
		ISP Sam sits down for dinner in a fine restaurant. The waiter, Carrier Ralph hands him a menu that reads "Chez Voice Network" with a graphic of a chef with a phone to his ear. He opens the menu revealing only 1 item "Cheeseburger $6.95". He looks puzzled.
		
		Stylish "cinema verite" interview setups with pertinent interviewees and relevant B-roll.
		
		A framed sign on a post reads "Maison de la Internet Thruway – New Menu, Better service". A camera move reveals the two men walking out of the restaurant doors patting their bellies after a good meal. They stop, turn and reach to shake hands.
		
		CU of shaking hands – slo-mo.
		
		CUT to CUs to reveal crossed fingers behind each back. Fingers uncross on the line "internet thruway can make it happen. [optional]
		
		FADE OUT.

SCENE	AUDIO	VIDEO

4.0	Business Case "Collaborate"
	
	NARRATOR:
	In racing, the crew needs teamwork and dedication to get to the winner's circle. In the race to win new customers, a dedicated crew of ISPs and carriers are needed to build the new data network. What's waiting in the winner's circle? Revenue enhancing services for both...
	
	INTERCUT ISP & CARRIER INTERVIEWEES:
	Addresses:
	   Streamlining operations without killing each others market
	   New service creation-new revenue opportunities
	   Cost savings for ISPs (up to 30%)
	   Easily scaled allocation of ports/bandwidth
	
	NARRATOR:
	With Internet Thruway, ISPs and carriers can collaborate to create revenue opportunities with new services. ISPs already using Internet Thruway have reduced operating costs by up to 30% by outsourcing the modem pool. And, capital constraints are relieved by converting the modem pool costs into a monthly expense. Carriers are having fun too, offering ISPs scalable bandwidth and new services while increasing customer satisfaction. Hey, this working together stuff can be fun and profitable.
		FADE IN
		TITLE SUPER: "Collaborate"
		
		A multi segmented screen shows racing footage, pit crew shots, 3d animation of the Nortel Indy Car, close ups shots of ISP Sam and Carrier Ralph in pit crew garb, working together. Close ups of tools, meters, and thumbs up. (possibly use new Nortel car in Orlando)
		
		Stylish "cinema verite" interview setups with pertinent interviewees and relevant B-roll.
		
		Segmented screen continuing to show racing clips combined with Internet clips, relevant graphics with shots of web users, business activities, Carrier/ISP images. Images include an RPM meter that reads "Savings"- the needle rev's to 30%. Another LED meter reads "Customer Satisfaction" - pegs into the red zone.
		
		FADE OUT.

SCENE	AUDIO	VIDEO
5.0	Technical "How It Works" NARRATOR: It's a struggle generating new revenue opportunities from the existing network. The beauty of Internet Thruway is its digital infrastructure based on proven Nortel products already in use today. Internet Thruway's Network Intelligence brings new revenue opportunities and increased efficiency for Carriers, ISPs and Enterprise clients. The Internet Thruway Management System puts ISPs closer to their customers than ever before possible. It simplifies provisioning and enables surveillance of Thruway elements from a single graphical workstation. Ever found yourself dialing into your system to check for modem availability? The ITMS provides the data to monitor and maintain port usage along with detailed call statistics through an integrated network map. Modem Traffic Analysis Reports enable quick adjustments in modem capacity. Try doing that with your current system. The ITMS Graphical User Interface reduces training time and speeds up deployment. In addition, the software is designed to integrate into existing and future Operation Support Systems. The ITMS also features Centralized Home Gateway Management which enables global configuration changes and provisioning of Home Gateway Load Balancing. And with features like Peak Load Modem Service, ISPs can base pricing on time of day or load priority for appropriate clients.	FADE IN TITLE SUPER: "How It Works" Open on field of cows grazing (maybe Fearrington Village cows). A farmer walks along a fence carrying a pail of milk. Attached to a fence post is a rectangular camera- The Cow Cam. It has a label right on it "CowCam". It is pointed into the pasture toward the belties. CGI graphics showing technical layout and description: Overview diagram showing relationship of Carrier, ISP and Enterprise within the network. The CowCam is represented in the diagram as a little farm. The movement of data in the simulation is represented by 3-d wireframe cows moving along the network path from point to point Focus is directed to ISP and ITMS ITMS component fits into the picture in diagram which includes composites of B-roll of GUI Video Examples of ITMS screens Someone looking at a report Someone manning a workstation. (images driven by best b-roll we can get Within Diagram lines being added simulated by many branches all with cows trailing off

VisionFactory, Inc. © 1997

SCENE	AUDIO	VIDEO
5.0	The Internet Thruway Intelligent Network Controller allows carriers to define and market different grades of service to ISPs while making more efficient use of Internet gateways. The INC's Real-Time Service Quality Management (SQM) can adjust the modem port count to meet traffic requirements and enables Point to Point Protocol services in a shared environment. Now Carriers with Internet Thruway can turn up new circuits for ISPs and Enterprises whenever they need them. ISPs need circuits fast. 60-90 day waits for new lines can sink a company. Internet Thruway's Network Intelligence allows instant circuit availability. And Virtual Point of Presence Means a portable presence instantly and seamlessly. INTERCUT ISP & CARRIER INTERVIEWEES: Addresses: Functionality of INC and ITMS (Bob Henry address)The New Intelligent Network Routing Option offers ubiquitous network availability at a lower cost and will support SS7 in Mid 1998 New features, more choices. How will you take advantage of Internet Thruway?	INC diagram. Stylish "cinema verite" interview setups with pertinent interviewees and relevant B-roll. The cows in field. Moo's mix with modems. CU Laptop Screen. In a web browser is the video window of the CowCam. ISP Sam from front looks down at the screen. He reaches for the glass of milk on the desk, lifts it to his mouth, drinks and lowers it leaving a milk mustache. Screen freezes. Title Super: "GOT BANDWIDTH?" FADE OUT.

SCENE	AUDIO	VIDEO

6.0	Internet Thruway "Validate"
	
	NARRATOR:
	It takes a carrier class delivery of products to develop the infrastructure necessary to create the new public data network. Nortel knows this – they helped build the voice network we use today. And now, with Internet Thruway, customers are seeing the benefits of lower operating costs and revenue enhancing services.
	
	NORTEL & ANALYSIS INTERVIEWEES:
	Addressing:
	  Nortel offers true "carrier class" products
	  Address competition?
	  ITW with Access Node in 1998
	  Multi-vendor environment
	  Address need for ISPs & carrier to embrace ITW and work together
	
	NARRATOR:
	Any questions? Good...
		FADE IN
		TITLE SUPER: "Validate"
		
		Series of CU shots of brass gears. Slow camera moves and light changes glide across the precision parts of a complex machine-only later revealed to be music box.
		
		A polished ornate brass key is inserted into a slot and is turned, winding the machine.
		
		Stylish "cinema verite" interview setups with pertinent interviewees and relevant B-roll.
		
		A rosewood box opens from the front. As the hinged top rises a chrome object on a spring appears and begins to spin. It is an Internet Thruway emblem. The music box chimes in with playful version of the theme music as the logo spins and is reflected in a mirror.
		
		FADE OUT.

SCENE	AUDIO	VIDEO
7.0	Conclusion Segment "The Promise Delivered" NARRATOR: ISPs and carriers are at a crossroads. The quest- to deliver on the promise of the New Internet. Today is the day that vision and planning meet the technology that makes this all possible.	FADE IN. TITLE SUPER: "The Promise Delivered" Road level CU down the double yellow line. Two sets of shoes walk toward the camera and stop. The two businessmen walk up to a crossroads in the middle of wide-open county. They look at a highway sign that reads "Future" with three arrows pointing in different directions. One of the men looks down and sees a golden tinker toy hub lying on the ground, picks it up, and examines it. The other man looks over at it. CU face of ISP Sam against a blue sky. CU face of Carrier Ralph CU of Road sign indicating the future. (CGI against blue sky some white clouds)

	ALL INTERVIEWEES: (multiple voices)
	Addressing:
	  Revenue & customer satisfaction
	  The vision to make changes
	  Hint at future services with a new network architecture
	  Final blast of ISP/Carrier collaboration
		Stylish "cinema verite" interview setups with pertinent interviewees and relevant B-roll.

	NARRATOR: Are you ready to invest in a technology that helps you stand out in a crowd? Internet Thruway is the solution that gives you the advantage in an intensely competitive market. The New Internet awaits – the promise has been delivered. Are you ready?	Return to businessman at crossroads. Aerial pullback shot as the two men walk off into the future together. FADE OUT. ITW logo Nortel logo www.nortel.com/thruway END.

VisionFactory, Inc. © 1997

I.T. 2 Style Sheet   1.0

Thursday, January 15, 1998

VIGNETTES:

- ALL SCRIPTED PIECES ARE TO BE LETTERBOXED (combination of slight anamorphic squeeze and black borders)
- CINELOOK TO BE APPLIED AT THE TIME OF LETTERBOXING
- SHOT ON DVCAM WITH CINELOOK IN MIND (no hotspots, splashes of color)
- LIBERAL USE OF CU (spaghetti western feel when we can get away with it)
- SLO-MO WHEN APPROPRO
- CAMERA MOVES ALMOST SUBLIMINAL IN CU
- JIBS AND DOLLIES MOTIVATED (farmer along fence, jib at end)
- COLOR SCHEME TO EACH VIGNETTE (ex: amber-sepia for gypsy)

INTERVIEWS:

- NATURAL SETTING THAT FLYS WITH OLD INTERVIEWS
- ALTERNATE FACING ANGLES (half left, half right)
- BOTH LAV AND BOOM FOR EVERYONE
- MAIN CAMERA STATIC
- 2ND CAMERA FLOATING COVERAGE FOR EACH INTERVIEWEE (not for entire interview, but a good amount during small talk, kinetic shots, hands, etc.
- 2ND CAMERA FOOTAGE TO BE CINELOOKED TO B&W STOCK AND INTERCUT BETWEEN INTERVIEWEES AND QUESTIONS (includes swish pans, snap zooms, shots including monitor, camera lighting etc.)

visionfactory

March 25, 1998

Dave Jemmett, President
Winstar Goodnet

I'm Michael Worthington, a video producer representing VisionFactory. We will be conducting the interview regarding Nortel's Internet Thruway on this Thursday morning at 11am at your location. The following are advance questions that will form the content of your interview.

Internet Thruway Interview Questions
T. Give me a brief history of your company. Discuss your growth, current architecture, future plans.
T. Discuss some of the competitive pressures within the marketplace.
T. Discuss the relationship with your carrier; your general understanding of the working relationship between ISPs and carriers.
Q. How did you hear about ITW? What were your immediate thoughts on the product? Your impression of the creation of a new public data network architecture?
Q. Were your services limited before ITW?
Q. What are some of the services you offered customers before installing ITW? What revenue enhancing services can/are you offering now?
Q. From an ISP perspective, does taking away terminating hardware (modems) affect the perception of what an ISP is? Does it create an "identity crisis" as a service provider without modems in the closet.
Q. What words describe the impact of ITW on your business?
Q. What cost savings have you been able to measure with ITW?
Q. What key features of ITW help your business in efficiency, statistical analysis, and planning?
Q. Have you set up any "virtual" POPs yet?
Q. Have you been able to respond quicker to your client's needs with ITW? In what ways?
Q. Now that you're using the product, what are overall feelings about its impact on your business? (Good, not so good, future)
T. Address the competition. Do you feel ITW gives you an advantage in your marketplace?
Q. Do you agree that collaboration is the key to success in the ISP business? Is a technology like ITW worth rallying around – putting aside past issues between ISPs and carriers?
Q. What is your vision of the future of the internet? How do you plan to ensure your business wins?

Below is contact information in case you need to touch base with me before Thursday morning. We will be arriving at your office at 10am to setup (it takes approximately 30-45 minutes for us to prep the location). Thank you so much for allowing us to take some of your time to help benefit our client's project. We look forward to seeing you on Thursday.

Internet Thruway Video

Wardrobe Requirements

Scene 2:

ISP SAM CARRIER RALPH (both)	WARDRODE A -	Business attire (Grayish Business suit) Have 2 choices Nice shoes
YOUNG PROGRAMMER	Hip artsy threads	
GYPSY	Gypsy Attire	

Scene 3:

ISP SAM	WARDROBE A
CARRIER RALPH	WARDROBE A plus waiter's apron (We'll provide)

Scene 4:

ISP SAM CARRIER RALPH (both)	Racing jacket, racing cap (we'll provide)

Scene 5:

CARRIER RALPH	Overalls, flannel shirt, rubber boots (check to see what talent has)
ISP SAM	WARDROBE A

Scene 7:

ISP SAM	WARDROBE A
CARRIER RALPH	WARDROBE A

Figure 4-0-1: This animated music box was part of my favorite scene from the project. It was probably the most complex and beautiful animated pieces we had done to date, but unfortunately the entire scene was cut from the final production.

Figures 4-2 to 4 (following pages): Animated mockups of the Tinker Toy sequence from preproduction - children's toys depict the complexity of the data network.

Figures 4-5 to 10: Storyboard sketches for the project helped coordinate the animation, green screen, and live action footage.

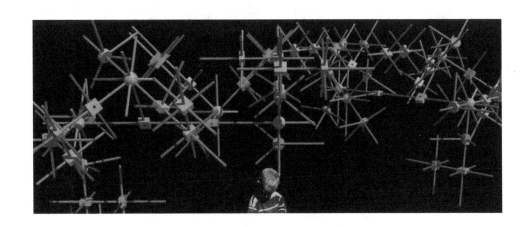

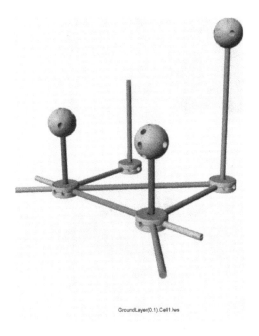

GroundLayer(0.1).Cell1.lws

visionfactory

Project . . . .
Client . . . .
Contact . . . .
. . . .
Version . . . .
Date . . . .
Artist . . . .
Art Director . . . .
Comments . . . .
. . . .
. . . .
. . . .
. . . .
. . . .
. . . .

© VisionFactory 1997

TWO GUYS WALKING TOWARDS CAMERA

MR TELCO + MR ISP WALKING UP TO
CROSSROADS OS

PAN UP TO SIGN

DISCOVERY OF TINKERTOY (PAN DOWN
FROM REACTION SHOT TO SIGN)

---

visionfactory

Project . . I.T.2 . . . .
Client . . NORTEL . . . .
Contact . . . .
. . . .
Version . . . .
Date . . . .
Artist . . . .
Art Director . . . .
Comments . . . .
. . . .
. . . .
. . . .
. . . .
. . . .
. . . .

© VisionFactory 1997

ESTABLISH CHILD PLAYING WITH
TINKER TOYS
DOLLY SHOTS

ECU'S OF TINKER TOYS

MOVING DOLLY SHOTS

ZOOM OUT TO REVEAL NETWORK

SHOTS OF PEOPLE USING
COMPUTERS; INTERNET
ISP EQUIPMENT ETC

visionfactory

Project . . . .
Client . . . .
Contact . . . .

Version . . . .
Date . . . .
Artist . . . .
Art Director . . . .
Comments . . . .

© VisionFactory 1997

visionfactory

Project . . . .
Client . . . .
Contact . . . .

Version . . . .
Date . . . .
Artist . . . .
Art Director . . . .
Comments . . . .

WOMAN REPLACED W/ TWO GUYS ⟶

© VisionFactory 1997

visionfactory

Project . . . .
Client . . . .
Contact . . . .
. . . .
Version . . . .
Date . . . .
Artist . . . .
Art Director . . . .
Comments . . . .

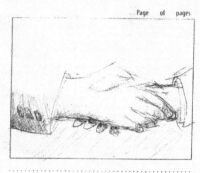

CHEESEBURGER
$6.95

© VisionFactory 1997

visionfactory

Project . . . .
Client . . . .
Contact . . . .
. . . .
Version . . . .
Date . . . .
Artist . . . .
Art Director . . . .
Comments . . . .

COWS GRAZING

FARMER WALKS THROUGH W/ MILK
PAIL

FARMER'S REACTION TO "STEER" LINE
- ALSO SHOT OF COW LOOKING PUZZLED TOO

VARIOUS GEAR + DRUM SHOTS

I.T. MUSIC BOX PLAYING

© VisionFactory 1997

Chapter 5: View Askew - HiddenMind
What if the world shifted 90 degrees counter-clockwise?

The 90's brought us the first interactive portable devices. Cell phones grew smaller and Palm devices were the hottest tools for personal information management. But for the really connected business person there was a new exciting tool that combined the best of both worlds – the Blackberry. With a Blackberry and other RIM devices, one could make all important business calls and communicate via text messages, and in an era when the App Store was still science fiction, a Blackberry could also run simple programs and share data with a central server.

Not far from the VisionFactory offices there was a company called HiddenMind that specialized in writing programs for the Blackberry. Their vision included productivity applications for mobile professionals that could access a central database, handle ordering and billing, look up schematics, interact with a help desk, and generally connect workers in the field to the resources back at home base. With the potential for a huge user base, and operating in a climate of readily available tech investment, Hidden Mind was well funded and was looking for an eye-catching trade show piece to attract new clients. They came to us to create a partially interactive presentation that would be presenter led.

The marketing team was young and full of ideas. Together we brainstormed on different ways to present something new. We wanted to show how the applications could operate in the real world and illustrate the value of the real-time interactivity. Showing the screen interfaces wasn't as important as showing the user solving a problem with their Blackberry, so we scripted a few scenarios that we thought made it very clear how HiddenMind could make a worker more productive. For a visual hook we decided on the somewhat crazy idea of shooting the video segments in a vertical aspect ratio. We would mount a large plasma screen on the tradeshow booth in a vertical orientation and set up a few rows of theater seating in front of it. A live host would gather a crowd at pre-determined times to introduce the video segments and present a sales pitch between our vignettes.

For the script we decided to get a little reflexive with our storyline – the piece became a movie within a movie featuring a production crew facing the challenge of shooting a commercial spot with a vertical aspect ratio. If this is getting confusing, well you'll just have to read the script. The idea was to let the audience in our little joke and take the opportunity to show how the characters used the HiddenMind software to solve some simple problems, saving time along the way.

The production was one of the more interesting pieces I worked on at VisionFactory. Although we had the hook of shooting with the camera on its side, it was pretty much a straight narrative fiction with continuity cuts, dialog and a number of locations. It's was a movie-style production with a small crew and tight schedule which went fairly smoothly apart from a small snag during the first morning of shooting. To achieve the 90 degree rotation of the camera, we had rented a Dutch tripod head that allows the camera to tilt side to side. The problem was that the head wouldn't quite tilt to 90 degrees, so with everyone still setting up the first shot, two of my crew members ran to a nearby machine shop where they fabricated an L shaped steel plate that we bolted to the tripod head and to the camera plate. Losing only about 30 minutes of production we were off and running with our one of a kind camera rig. I still have that plate in my camera kit just in case I get the call for another askew shoot.

The HiddenMind script written in the typical Hollywood screenplay format. A rule of thumb for this format is that a single page of script usually equates to around a minute of screen time. For the client, it is an easy format to review and suggest changes, and for the production team and actors it helps everyone to literally work from the same page. Personally I find it to be the easiest in which to work.

In this chapter I've included a character list and an original version of the HiddenMind script. Then there is a lined script from the actual shoot. This was the script that I used as I directed the piece. I thought it would interesting to include because it is a snapshot of how shots were selected during each scene, and shows some dialog changes and other details that were worked out at the actual time of shooting. To understand the vertical lines marked on the script you need to know a little about coverage.

Coverage refers to the amount of footage you shoot for a given scene or piece. In a Hollywood film, coverage usually refers to the number of angles you take of a single scene. Traditional film shoots involve a single camera that is moved around to get different camera shots (changes in angle and frame size like a wide shot, two shot, or close-up). This method requires the actors to play through a scene multiple times to get the right mix of performance and angles. The term continuity refers to how things must appear continuous between these many versions of the same scene. Continuity errors are sometimes apparent even in the most polished films. For example, a hand is up in the wide shot and down on the cut to close up. A wine glass appears magically in the two shot and is gone again in a close up. All of this can become very confusing when you are directing a scene, and the lined script is a visual way to keep up with the coverage. Each shot is marked with a vertical line directly over the portions of the script covered in that shot. This running tally is an excellent way to keep your head during the shoot, and when editing time comes, that document is a tremendous help.

——

HiddenMind

Cast:

Reporter – Alicia Airwave
Insurance Salesman – Actor Trent Jackknife
Insurance Customer – John Publicson
Pharmaceutical Rep. – Actress Lisa Lesser
Repairman – Robert Strongshake
Director – Cecil B. Radio
P.A.
Camera Man
Reporter's Cameraman

Devices:

Wireless phone
RIM (Blackberry)
Wireless PDA
Pager

Scene 1: Commercial Shoot – Insurance Salesman at client's office

Fade in:

Int. Executive Office – Day

Surrounding this professional's office is the equipment and crew of a video production. The room is decorated with light stands, flags, a camera crew, director and production assistant. At the center of the room, two actors are seated across from one another at a table.

One odd thing about the scene is immediately apparent. The shot is on it's side. Since our presentation screen is vertical or portrait (instead of landscape), the image appears to be ninety degrees off.

In this canted state the following occurs:

Hands hold a clapper to the camera.

                              P.A.
                  HiddenMind, scene 15 take 34.

                                      Director
                  And... action

The clapper is pulled and the camera begins to dolly toward the table.

                                      Director
                  Cut.

Vertical Angle

Wider view is of the director and crew. The production assistant is showing the director something.

Tighter on the two.

                                    PA
                  They want to use a vertical screen.

                                      Director
                  They what?

The PA shows the director his PDA.

                                    PA
                  Vertical. They want to turn it on it's side.

Close up on the HiddenMind powered PDA. It shows a diagram of a LCD screen. The image on the PDA animates from normal landscape view to a vertically oriented view.

FREEZE FRAME

The close up of the PDA freezes, tints a SELECTED COLOR, and ZOOMS CLOSER as KEYWORDS animate onscreen.

Keywords here:
HiddenMind
Work Smarter,
Not Harder

As dramatically as they tumbled onscreen the graphics scurry off.

Wide

The director steps up and announces:

Director

Ok everybody. We're going to make some adjustments here.

Jump cuts:

Camera man adjusting tripod
Actors guided to sit closer by director
Tilting of camera
Continuity shot of Camera POV righting the image

The Director approaches the actors.

Director

Trent baby. It's great, just great. This time look at your PDA. All of the insurance rates are there. Real time, right from your office database. Remember, this is HiddenMind Technology. Always on, seamless. Got it?

Trent

Seamless. Got it.

The director returns to his seat. Beside him is the camera, in front of him is a monitor with the camera's image.

Director

Ready and………….

He cocks his head sideways at the monitor. Now the image on the monitor is off by ninety degrees.

Director (cont.)

Hold it.

The director looks to the PA, gives him a nod toward the monitor.

Reverse – The PA hurries to turn the monitor on its side, righting the image.

Director gives a thumbs up.

> **Director**
>
> Action.

CUT TO REPORTER CAM

At the edge of the production is Alicia Airwave - microphone wielding reporter. Behind her the scene is being filmed, Perhaps too there is a monitor beside her showing the action being captured behind her. The crew captures a slow dolly in to the table.

> **Alicia**
>
> Hi, I'm Alicia Airwave for the Wireless Entertainment Network. Today, from the set of their new corporate video, we feature HiddenMind, the revolutionary provider of next generation wireless solutions for mobile and remote professionals.

In classic news reporter fashion, the HiddenMind logo supers beside Alicia's shoulder.

CUT TO

Fullscreen of the shots being created by the video crew. Alicia's VO continues. Shot pushes toward the insurance salesman showing his customer the data streaming in on his PDA. Close Up of the PDA shows the terms and rate for business liability insurance updating instantly.

> **Alicia**
>
> Through its HiddenLogic platform, HiddenMind solutions extend a company's network to mobile professionals like this insurance agent. On demand, he can access up-to-date rates and to provide a competitive quote for his client. When timing is critical to making a deal, applications built on the HiddenLogic platform provide the instant connection and computing power needed by mobile professionals.

The agent and his customer shake hands. The Shot includes the PDA on the table.

FREEZE FRAME

> **HANDSHAKE AND PDA zooms forward. Keywords animate in.**
>
> **Keywords:**
> **HiddenLogic**
> **Flexible**

Scalable
Platform
As dramatically as they tumbled onscreen the graphics scurry off.

Wide shot on Crew

Director stands as he yells.

                              Director
          Cut.

Crew activity includes cameraman checking the camera. Makeup walks to Actors.

The PA approaches the director. She shows him the her PDA.

Close up on PDA

It has two headshots on it.

                              PA
          Here are the choices for tomorrows shoot.

The Director clicks on one with a stylus. It glows as it is selected.

                              Director
          He's the one.

FREEZE FRAME

     Tint and zoom in on hand on the PDA

     **This still slides into a slot while two other stills from this sequence also
     animate in. The resulting frame is   a stack of three tinted freezes of the PDA
     interactions.**

     Keywords:
     HiddenMessenger
     Always on
     Group messaging
     Efficient
     Convenient

     As dramatically as they tumbled onscreen the graphics scurry off.

Scene 2 – HiddenMind exposition section

Ext. HiddenMind Headquarters – Day

Alicia Airwave and her cameraman stand by the sign for HiddenMind. Alicia holds a mirror and is checking her hair. Cameraman hands her a microphone and she focuses on the lens as he steadies for a shot.

CAMERA SHOT

Alicia stares into the lens.

> Alicia
>
> Three…two……(beat).
> HiddenMind technologies help corporations to work smarter, not harder.
> But how do they do it? We're at HiddenMind headquarters to find out.

Int. HiddenMind Headquarters – Day

This section is made up of a series of interview clips and b-roll shots that explain the core technologies of HiddenMind and expound on the significant partnerships HiddenMind has developed.

This section runs about 1:30.

Ext. HiddenMind Headquarters – Day

Alicia addresses the camera.

> Alicia
>
> A revolutionary platform for wireless applications and strong partnerships. That's
> why HiddenMind is changing the way mobile professionals do business.

Alicia holds in the frame, smiling.

Wider – on Alicia and Cameraman. She holds, then breaks her stare.

> Alicia
>
> Great.

A beeper rings. Alicia checks her pocket, pulls out the device and looks at it.

> Alicia
>
> Here are the directions to the next shoot. Let's go.

She tosses the device to Biff, her cameraman. He catches it and looks at the display.

CLOSE UP DISPLAY

> *1400 West Greene St.*

Second house on the right.
{directions}

FREEZE FRAME

        Tint and zoom in on the image of the beeper. And other devices also slide into the graphic. Keywords animate in.

        Keywords:
        Bla bla bla

        As dramatically as they tumbled onscreen the graphics scurry off.

Scene 3 – The Drug Rep and the Repairman

Ext. Drug Rep's Back Porch – Day

CLOSE UP CLAPPER

PA

Hidden Mind Scene 28b take 47.

Smack. The clapper claps. The PA pulls it from the frame revealing a wide shot of the porch where Lisa Lesser, the pharmaceutical rep, and Bob Strongshake – AC Repairman are chatting. Each holds a Blackberry device. The shot pushes in very slowly.

Reverse – the production camera pushes dead toward us. Director is off to the side, calling direction.

Director

Ok, Bob, you've got to check on that air conditioner part. You are pulling it up from the database. And Lisa, you are accessing your office scheduling software.

Now kiss.

WIDE – PRODUCTION TEAM

We see the scene as this camera pulls back revealing Alicia Airwave at the edge of the set.

Alicia

Back on the set of the HiddenMind video, today we look at how the HiddenLogic platform extends a company's network to increase productivity and efficiency.

PRODUCTION CAMERA SHOTS

Medium shots of Lisa and Bob. Close ups of Blackberry devices. Close ups of faces.

Alicia (VO)

As a Pharmaceutical Rep., Lisa relies on up to date scheduling
to manage her time in the field. With HiddenMind, her
appointments and cancellations are constantly updated and at
her fingertips. Plus she can access product information over
the network instantly. Bob also takes advantage of his company's
to check inventory and pricing information.

Bob and Lisa refer to their respective devices.

                                 Bob
                I can have the part here by two o'clock.

                                 Lisa
        Great. My 1:30 was cancelled, so I'm meet you back here at two.

FREEZE FRAME

**Tint and zoom on the two. Two other freezes – one of Lisa's Blackberry and
one of Bob's slide into the composition.**

Keywords:
HiddenMind
On the go
Always connected
Intuitive
Wired
And
Wireless

Scene 4 – Wrap up Section

Ext. Impressive and cool location – Day

Alicia stands at this cool location to wrap up her behind the scenes look at HiddenMind. As
she talks a series of imagery from the video, the stills, and the text messaging animate
through a three paned vertical canvas.

                                Alicia
            Offering flexible and scalable next generation wireless solutions,
            including the HiddenLogic platform and applications like
            HiddenMessenger, HiddenMind has revolutionized how
            mobile professionals communicate and access technology.
            HiddenMind solutions put the power of your company's network
            and software resources in the hands of every employee, regardless
            of their location. For 24,7,365 access to data, applications, and
            your enterprise infrastructure there is only one choice. HiddenMind.

Animated montage of graphics end on the HiddenMind logo.

Fade out.

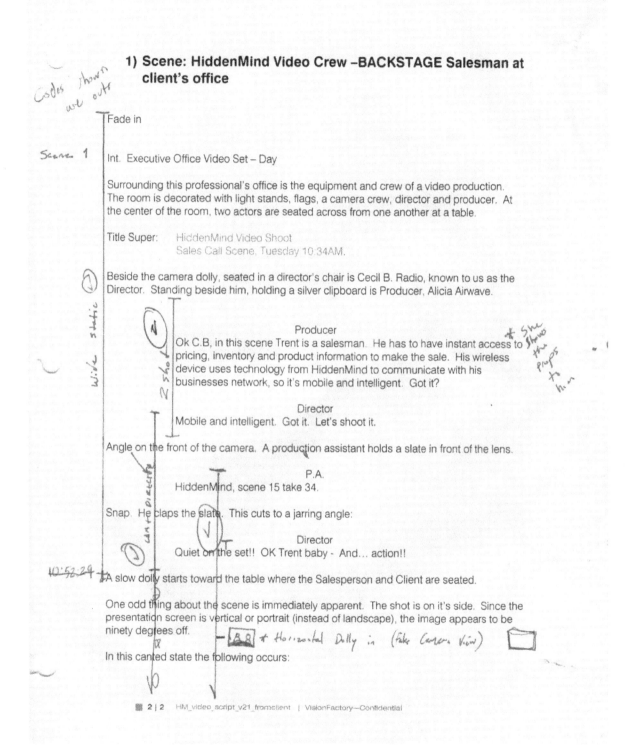

1) Scene: HiddenMind Video Crew –BACKSTAGE Salesman at client's office

Codes shown not out

Fade in

Scene 1

Int. Executive Office Video Set – Day

Surrounding this professional's office is the equipment and crew of a video production. The room is decorated with light stands, flags, a camera crew, director and producer. At the center of the room, two actors are seated across from one another at a table.

Title Super: HiddenMind Video Shoot
                Sales Call Scene, Tuesday 10:34AM.

wide static

Beside the camera dolly, seated in a director's chair is Cecil B. Radio, known to us as the Director. Standing beside him, holding a silver clipboard is Producer, Alicia Airwave.

2 shot

                        Producer
Ok C.B, in this scene Trent is a salesman. He has to have instant access to pricing, inventory and product information to make the sale. His wireless device uses technology from HiddenMind to communicate with his businesses network, so it's mobile and intelligent. Got it?

+ she shows the props to him

                        Director
Mobile and intelligent. Got it. Let's shoot it.

Angle on the front of the camera. A production assistant holds a slate in front of the lens.

un-directed

                        P.A.
HiddenMind, scene 15 take 34.

Snap. He claps the slate. This cuts to a jarring angle:

                        Director
Quiet on the set!! OK Trent baby - And... action!!

10:52:29 A slow dolly starts toward the table where the Salesperson and Client are seated.

One odd thing about the scene is immediately apparent. The shot is on it's side. Since the presentation screen is vertical or portrait (instead of landscape), the image appears to be ninety degrees off. — [A.B] + Horizontal Dolly in (fake Camera View)

In this canted state the following occurs:

■ 2 | 2   HM_video_script_v21_fromclient | VisionFactory—Confidential

Figure 5-1: The next several pages include my copy of the HiddenMind script with shots lined on each scene and some changes scribbled during the shoot.

A "HiddenMind ring" chimes out.

Producer grabbing her device and looks at screen…

> **Producer**
> Wait, wait, wait…… I'm getting another script update.

> **Director**
> Cut. What is it now?

Vertical Angle

Wider view is of the director and crew. The Producer is showing the Director something.

Tighter on the two. She has a device in her hand. It looks like a PDA.

> **Producer**
> They want to use a vertical screen.

> **Director**
> They what?

The Producer shows the director her Blackberry (large screen model).

> **Producer**
> Vertical. They want to turn it on it's side.

GRAPHIC (superimposed animation)

Close up on the HiddenMind powered Blackberry. It shows a form with the words "Change Order" at the top and a diagram of a LCD screen mounted vertically on a tradeshow booth below. The Producer scrolls down to reveal a button that says "Accept Change."

> **Producer**
> Get it? We've got to change the way we're shooting.

> **Director**
> Good thing we found out now. How smart! We could have wasted this whole shoot. It would be really hard to go back and shoot this all over again. Phew…. Thank goodness for cutting edge wireless technology!

> **Producer**
> Just remember CB the client is always right, the client is always right! (smiles knowingly – once again, she has saved the director)

Director

Got it, the Client is always right.

The Director looks at the producer who shakes her head in agreement.

Music cue: Jazzy beat starts, motivating a graphic sequence:

[handwritten in right margin: Prod (cont) ... Director (cont) ... Nice Frame For Freeze/Zoom]

2) Scene: Freeze Frame A

The close up of the PDA freezes, tints a SELECTED COLOR, and ZOOMS CLOSER as KEYWORDS animate onscreen.

Keywords here:
HiddenMind
Creating Mobile Intelligence

As dramatically as they tumbled onscreen the graphics scurry off.

Jazzy music continues.

[handwritten checkmark in circle]

3) Scene: HiddenMind Video Crew – BACKSTAGE - Salesman at client's office

Wide of the set and crew

The director stands up and announces:

Director

Ok everybody. We just got some new info, so we're going to make some adjustments here.

[handwritten: He walks Toward the Actors]

Jump cuts:

- Camera man adjusting tripod
- Actors guided to sit closer by director
- Tilting of camera
- Continuity shot of Camera POV righting the image *[handwritten: (Actors and Set Dresser)]*

The Director approaches the actors.

Director

Trent baby. It's great, just great. This time look at your Blackberry. All of the rates and data are there – updated in real time!!. That's Real time baby, right from your office database. Remember, this is HiddenMind Technology.

[handwritten margin notes: 3 shot ... (cut in cut)]

4 | 4   HM_video_script_v21_fromclient | VisionFactory—Confidential

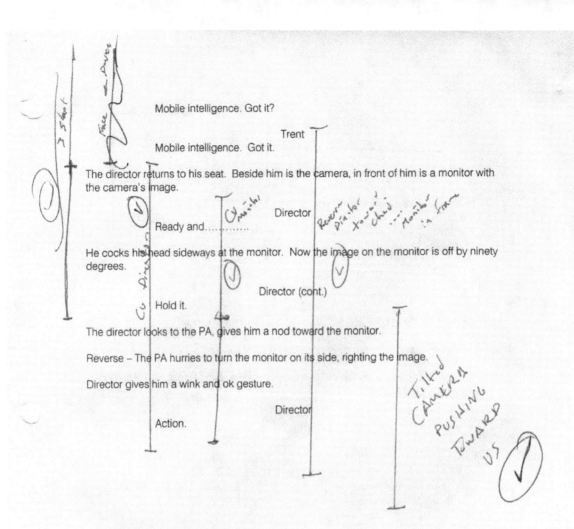

Mobile intelligence. Got it?

                                        Trent

Mobile intelligence. Got it.

The director returns to his seat. Beside him is the camera, in front of him is a monitor with the camera's image.

                                        Director

Ready and.............

He cocks his head sideways at the monitor. Now the image on the monitor is off by ninety degrees.

                                        Director (cont.)

Hold it.

The director looks to the PA, gives him a nod toward the monitor.

Reverse – The PA hurries to turn the monitor on its side, righting the image.

Director gives him a wink and ok gesture.

                                        Director

Action.

4) Scene: HiddenMind Commercial PRODUCTION CAMERA VIEW

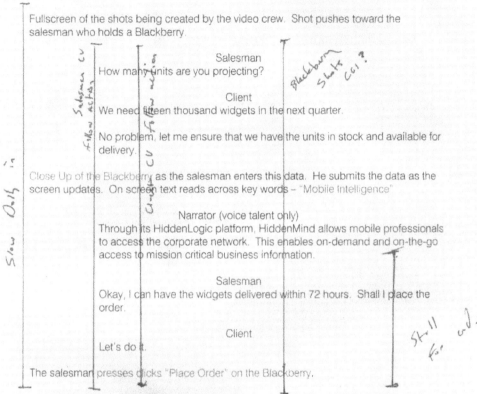

Fullscreen of the shots being created by the video crew. Shot pushes toward the salesman who holds a Blackberry.

Salesman
How many units are you projecting?

Client
We need fifteen thousand widgets in the next quarter.

No problem, let me ensure that we have the units in stock and available for delivery.

Close Up of the Blackberry as the salesman enters this data. He submits the data as the screen updates. On screen text reads across key words – "Mobile Intelligence"

Narrator (voice talent only)
Through its HiddenLogic platform, HiddenMind allows mobile professionals to access the corporate network. This enables on-demand and on-the-go access to mission critical business information.

Salesman
Okay, I can have the widgets delivered within 72 hours. Shall I place the order.

Client
Let's do it.

The salesman presses clicks "Place Order" on the Blackberry.

5) Scene: FREEZE FRAME B

Blackberry image zooms forward. Keywords animate in.

Keywords:
HiddenMind "Creating Mobile Intelligence"
HiddenLogic
Work Smarter.
Not Harder

Narrator

HiddenMind's wireless software allows businesses – from IT managers to application developers to mobile professionals – to work smarter, not harder.

As dramatically as they tumbled onscreen the graphics scurry off.

6) Scene: HiddenMind Interview – Video Crew

Ext. Car – Day

The producer and director arrive at HiddenMind and are walking in and having a conversation.

Title Super: HiddenMind Headquarters
Interview Shoot, Wednesday 9:00 AM

Producer
OK, we are here to shoot a straight interview, correct? Where is our crew?

Director
They'll be here.

Producer
CB, where are they?

Director grabs his phone and begins pushing buttons on the key pad.

Narrator
HiddenMessenger Group Messaging – for the HiddenLogic platform - allows users to establish and maintain groups for text-based messaging from any SMS-enabled device.

The "HiddenMind chime" rings out. The Director looks at his Nokia phone.

Director
Just received a reply... they are 15 minutes away. Just finishing up another shoot. They should be here soon.

Producer
That's fine, let's go in and meet the founder of HiddenMind. I'm interested to see what this company is all about anyways

Director
Got it. Whoops sorry...

7) Scene: FREEZE FRAME C

Handwritten annotations:
- Pull Dolly
- Wide shot
- Actors walk to zoom
- STOP DOLLY
- CU Director / Phone
- Actors
- Producer walks around from Passenger Side. Director is closing door. → Walking → Stop
- shot
- smile for the freeze frame

Tint and zoom in on Blackberry.

Keywords:
HiddenMind "Creating Mobile Intelligence"
HiddenMessenger
Group messaging

As dramatically as they tumbled onscreen the graphics scurry off.

8) Scene: HiddenMind Headquarters – Interview

This section is made up of a series of interview clips of HiddenMind's founder. These clips explain the core technologies of HiddenMind and explain the vision that HM has for wireless technology.

Each answer is followed by a sliding graphic bumper that includes keywords of the next question. The Same Jazzy beat from before helps move this process along.

Consisting of 3-5 short answers, this section runs about one minute.

The last assemblage of graphic s include a variety of partner logos and keywords.

Narrator
HiddenMind Technology, founded on the idea of making wireless work for the people that do the work!

As dramatically as they tumbled onscreen the graphics scurry off.

9) Scene : HiddenMind Video Crew – BACKSTAGE - The Drug Rep and the Repairman

9

INT. Drug Rep's Kitchen – Day

The spacious kitchen and connected den are populated by the film crew and production equipment. At the kitchen counter are two actors portraying a pharmaceutical rep. and a refrigerator repairman. The Producer and Director stand beside the camera. Shots of the actors reviewing their scripts intercut with the scene.

Title Super: Home of Pharmaceutical Rep., Weds, 3:00 PM

                                    Producer
Lisa is a Pharmaceutical Rep. She relies on up to date data and communications to efficiently manage her time in the field. With HiddenMind, she can manage most administrative tasks from her wireless device giving her more time to spend in the field. Bob's here to repair the fridge. He takes advantage of his company's database to check inventory and pricing information. This is about being more productive and efficient when doing business.

                                    Director
Got it. Productivity and efficiency. You know, this HiddenMind stuff is really cool. I've got to tell my agent about it. (TURNS TO CREW) People! Let's get ready – where is Bob?

ANGLE ON CAMERA

The director is seated beside the camera.

                                    Director
Ok, Bob baby, you've got to check on that refrigerator part.
You are pulling it up from the database. And Lisa, you're finishing off an expense report.

PA slides the slate into the frame.

                                    PA
Hidden Mind Scene 28b take 47.

Smack. The clapper claps. The PA pulls it from the frame. The production camera pushes dead toward us.

10)   Scene: HiddenMind Video Crew: PRODUCTION
CAMERA SHOTS

Lisa Lesser, the pharmaceutical rep, and Bob Strongshake – AC Repairman are chatting. Lisa holds a Blackberry device and Bob has a Motorola phone. The shot pushes in very slowly.

Medium shots of Lisa and Bob.

Bob
Just let me check to see if the part is available. Gimme one second.

Lisa
No problem, I'll just send in this expense report from lunch, while I wait.

Close ups of Bob's cell phone. He's entering a part number.

Close up of Lisa's Blackberry. She communicates her "Expense Report."

The "HiddenMind chime" rings out.

Lisa pulls up HiddenMessenger Group Messaging on her cell phone with the message "I'll cover your 2 – JB."

Narrator
Creating wireless software technology that is scalable, flexible and powerful, HiddenMind enables any mobile professional to manage their time and resources more efficiently.

Bob and Lisa refer to their respective devices.

Bob
I can have the part here by two o'clock.

Lisa looks up from her phone.

Lisa
Great. My teammate just said he could cover my two o'clock. I'll meet you back here then.

11)   SCENE: FREEZE FRAME D

Tint and zoom on the two. Three other freezes – one of Lisa's Blackberry, one of Lisa's phone and one of Bob's phone slide into the composition.

Keywords:
HiddenMind "Creating Mobile Intelligence"
Intuitive
Efficient
Productive

Narrator
By placing the power of the network in the hands of mobile
professionals, HiddenMind improves productivity
and customer service while reducing the cost of doing business.

12)   Scene – Conclusion

Collage of HiddenMind powered imagery from the previous scenes.

A series of imagery from the video, the stills, and the text messaging animate through a three paned vertical canvas.

Narrator
Offering flexible and scalable next generation wireless software,
including the HiddenLogic platform and applications like
HiddenMessenger, HiddenMind is revolutionizing how
mobile professionals communicate and use technology to access data.
HiddenMind solutions put the power of the network and into the hands of
the people in the field. For 24, 7, 365 access to data, applications, and
your enterprise infrastructure there is only one choice. HiddenMind.

Animated montage of graphics end on the HiddenMind logo.

Fade out.

AE

FINAL   SCENE

HM Sound.

2 shot Prod + Dir.

Prod looks down. Then up.

"They want the whole thing in 3-D."

DIRECTOR BLANK, TURNS TO CAMERA.

" 3D. Got it. "   [BLACK .]

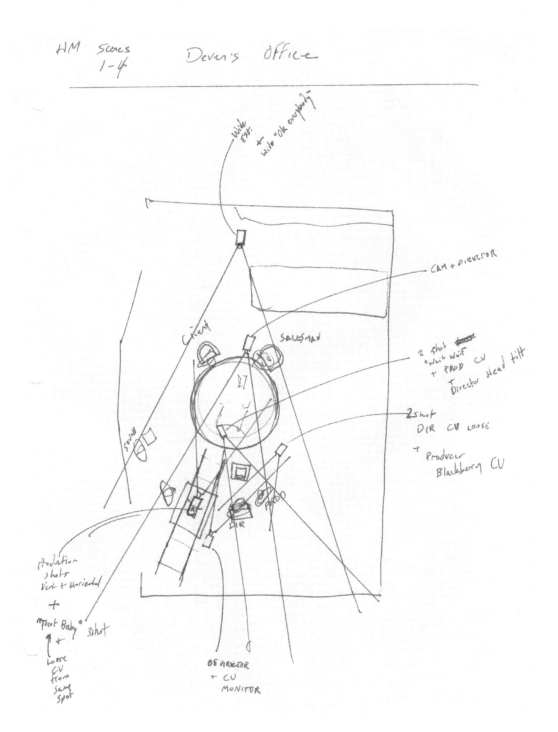

Figures 5- 2 to 5: Sketches made for the HiddenMind video show the camera angles for particular scenes. This was used to help create the lighting and actor block as well as coordinate camera moves. Each set of conical lines represents a different camera position and lens coverage approximation.

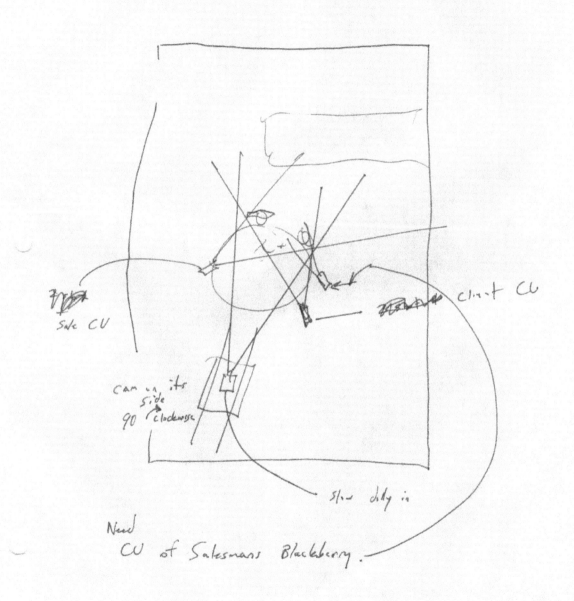

Side CU

Client CU

Cam on its side
90° clockwise

Slow dolly in

Need
CU of Salesmans Blackberry.

DEVENS HOUSE   SCENES   9-10

#10 DENMIND

- ☑ MASTER EST
- ☐ OS DIRECTOR
- ☑ INTO CAMERA
- ☑ OVERHEAD PROD + DIRECTOR

OVERHEAD EST

①

②

BUILDING DIRECTOR

2 shot + CU PROD / DIRECTOR LOSE

PROD

DIRE

④

③

BOB

K

INTO FAKE CAMERA

KITCHEN

84

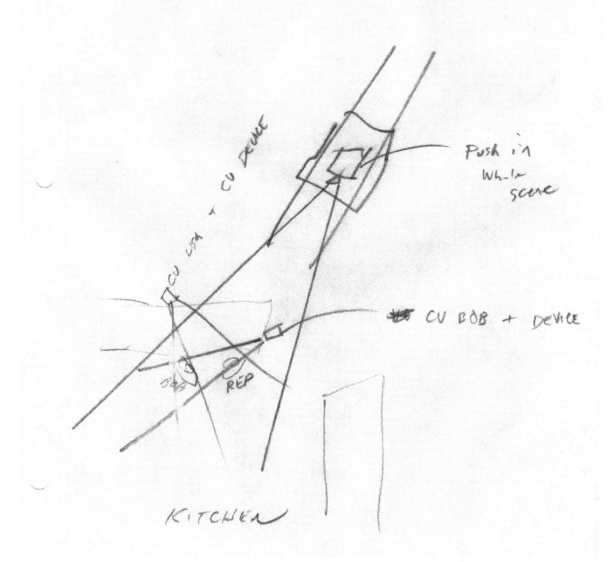

Chapter 6: DNN
Opening the floodgates

At VisionFactory we were always excited about naming things. I think that the first thing that made something "new" and our own was to give it a catchy name. It also showed the client that we were actually doing something for the money they paid us. Project names might be the title of the video we were about to do, a shorthand code for an interactive project or an all-encompassing phrase for a group of work for a certain client. Some names would become marketable products of their own, like "i-Nav", or "e-Space", or the ambitious, visionary, yet horribly named "Mediatation". Even the process of coming up with VisionFactory was a sort of in-house competition. All of these individual creative types battled for the best replacement for what we had decided was a dull name – Digital Imagery. Our first web address was www.dimagery.com. The very thought of that being typed in by a prospective client gives me chills now, plus the idea of Digital Imagery didn't capture our interactive nature or our film and video aspirations. We wanted something that showed we were visionaries. We were the place to go to when a client wanted something new and exciting. And we were producers, taking a raw idea and churning out a final product that wowed its audience. We were the Vision Factory. Fortunately the timing was right and the web address was available.

The pride of naming something new carried over into a long shot proposal for a Nortel client responsible for managing the Executive Briefing Center at the nearby Nortel headquarters. This EBC was a meeting area for prospective Nortel customers. It consisted of several conference rooms and a reception area. The client had been given the task to expand this area into a true showcase. Her vision was one of a customer experience where visiting groups would be treated to a journey through Nortel solutions and then lead to the meeting space where they would have every luxury while the Nortel sales staff convinced them to invest in really expensive solutions. For us, the likelihood of even being asked to bid on a job of this scope was slim, so when we were given the opportunity, we jumped in with every resource we had. We knew this could become a multi-million dollar job. What did we name it? "Destination Nortel Networks".

We spent probably two solid weeks with about 12 staff members focused entirely on putting together the Destination Nortel Networks (DNN for short) proposal. The idea was to create a visitor experience in several stages, choreographed and scheduled so the sales force could weave through an elaborate space, showing the high tech Nortel networking solutions and software platforms to a captive audience. It would be a cross between Disney World and the Star Trek Bridge. We described futuristic screen devices, a theater with a retracting wall, and interactive stations for small groups or individuals. The sound design was specified, the types of content were touched on, and even the arrangement of the conference rooms and the furniture was described. The vision was grand and expensive, and beyond the physical creation of the space, there was the key to it all - about 2 million dollars of media production that told the Nortel Networks story.

The document that we created was a masterpiece, but we knew that our small company would be up against giants that had been working within the Briefing Center space for years. We had no track record working on anything close to the size of this project. We knew the only thing we could do was to translate our vision into a media piece to present along with the proposal. We decided to visualize the concept with a series of 3D walkthroughs cut to a professional; narrator and music bed. This would be presented on three large projection screen s to the Nortel team on the day of the proposals. Our main animator got to work in LightWave 3D and we crafted a narration track that was concise but filled with crucial points. We pushed the theme of our title "Destination Nortel Networks", as it was imperative that the client understood that we had been listening. The piece had to reflect all of the ideas we had created together. Their buy-in during the proposal process was another of our advantages. It was key that we showed our company as a partner in creation, rather than a dictator of what they should be doing.

One strength of our approach was the modularity of the design. The experience could be linear, or free flowing. The media could be standard or customized. A particular group could have an entirely tailored trip through this technological amusement park, and we would be the partner that could make that happen.

Our efforts paid off. The gamble had worked. After the round of companies presented their proposals, and the selection team mulled the pros and cons of each, we were informed that we had been chosen for the project. The client knew we had the least experience and were the smallest, but they also knew that we had put in the most effort and created the most compelling vision. They were looking for a partner and we fit the bill. Needless to say, we were elated, but we also realized that now we had to actually create what we had dreamed up. In a celebratory instant, we knew we'd have to double in size, hiring every talented developer we could find. The floodgates were open and were had to start swimming fast.

The following list is a menu of the media items we had to create for DNN. Any single piece would have been a nice little project for the old VisionFactory. With all combined into a single project however, we knew it was time to streamline our process, look for economies of scale and get to work checking off completed pieces. The list is broken down into sections that were the different stops along the DNN experience. Some pieces were part of an interactive menu, and some were experienced by the entire group. The idea of a visitor using a membership card was part of our original idea, and it opened up the possibility of a one-to-one experience for each visitor. It also allowed a post visit relationship to exist between the sales team and the visitor, cataloging his or her interests and media selections. These were fairly new concepts when we were creating DNN.

As you can imagine from looking at the list, DNN represented an enormous amount of production. This included live action videos and a great number of animated pieces. In order to take on this much work we expanded our ranks, hiring several new programmers, animators, producers and editors. There were growing pains, but the common sense of purpose and deadline driven target kept the machine rolling and brought out some of our most creative work. In the end, the group produced approximately 2 million dollars of budgeted media to fill the space for the grand opening.

DNN Media List:

Portal
- 2 full screen digital videos (90 seconds each)
    Wonder World
    What the Future Used to Be

Theater
- 1 video (5-7 minutes)

Hub
- 16 full screen digital video clips (45-60 sec each) – listed below
    Centrex Vision
    Centrex Features and Benefits
    Centrex Components
    Centrex Solutions
    Succession Vision
    Succession Features and Benefits
    Succession Components

Succession Solutions
Signaling Vision
Signaling Features and Benefits
Signaling Components
Signaling Solutions
Integrated Wireless Vision
Integrated Wireless Features and Benefits
Integrated Wireless Components
Integrated Wireless Solutions

InfoNode

- 16 'title' pages with high level content addressing the following (format to be determined):

  Centrex Vision
  Centrex Features and Benefits
  Centrex Components
  Centrex Solutions
  Succession Vision
  Succession Features and Benefits
  Succession Components
  Succession Solutions
  Signaling Vision
  Signaling Features and Benefits
  Signaling Components
  Signaling Solutions
  Integrated Wireless Vision
  Integrated Wireless Features and Benefits
  Integrated Wireless Components
  Integrated Wireless Solutions

- Four network diagrams (1 for each solution set)
- 15-20 still images related to content
- Fifty 15-30 second video clips (mpgs) for Everybody's Talking (10-15 per solution set)
- 40-50 Pdf files

Succession:

6 product sheets
1 brochure
2 white paper
1 backgrounder

Centrex Unlimited

1 Overview

Call Center

1 Overview
6 Product sheets

Centrex VABD

        1 product sheet

Centrex IP

        1 product sheet
        1 white paper

Integrated Wireless

        1 Overview
        1 brochure for carriers

1 Meg Modem

        1 Overview
        1 product brief

Signaling Solutions

        2 planners
        7 brochures
        7 product sheets

Nortel Generic

        1 corporate brochure

SimSpace

- 4 Simulation experiences – 1 for each solution set – the experience may be 1 long, detailed simulation or 3-4 mini simulations/demonstrations (Director/Flash, etc)

Included here are some of the scripts that were created for the DNN pieces. The wide variety of content called for different approaches to the scripts. Some of the content was interactive and others were linear video. The goal was to have all pieces working from a common library of graphical elements, music and general style in order to make the DNN experience more impactful.

The DNN Primer Video

As part of the theater experience for the visitors, we created what we called the Primer video, an instructional piece describing the many features and different areas of DNN. This was a mix of 3D and live action footage showing visitors interacting within the space. The Primer was also an outgrowth of the original concept video we had created to sell our vision of the space. The entire DNN experience was designed as sort of a tech

90

amusement park. The space was designed to flow to create an immersive user experience, and the Primer video was the tutorial for this experience.

The two column script format for this piece was the easiest way to convey to the director, narrator, animator and editor how the mix of live action footage, motion graphics and 3d footage would flow. The layout allowed the team to work from a common place to create the individual elements and determine rough timing. It was the director and editor's job to work out the final timing and flow in the edit suite.

DNN was a huge project, and the Primer was one of the first pieces that the visitors to the center would see. This required a high end approach to the piece. The graphic design, animations and live action footage were some of the best we'd done to date. This was a showcase piece for Nortel and by extension for us.

September 17, 1999

Audio	Video
Welcome to the Nortel Networks Executive Briefing Center in RTP, North Carolina. This application-rich experience will put you directly in touch with the power of Nortel Networks solutions that enable Unified Networks.	Shot of reception area with sign "Executive Briefing Center" mixed with shots of NC-2 façade (w/ "Nortel Networks" signage and garden area.)
The Center is a SMART environment. The system design reconfigures the delivery, content, and context of a message based on an individual visitor to provide a meaningful, unique experience for each person.	Visitor swiping card Screen says "Welcome Joe Bob"
Narration Your visit will continue in the Hub, a viewing station for full-screen digital video clips. You will be presented with a customized menu of applications and solution sets at one of the five custom touch screen kiosks within a sound dome for the ultimate audio/visual experience. Groups may view the videos via a large, overhead plasma display. Here you build a foundation of knowledge, upon which you can investigate the solution sets further throughout the Center.	In a seating position, from the middle front seat inside the theater looking out into the HUB. The screen has slid completely to the left and the opening into the HUB is completely open and undisturbed. Looping Nortel Networks logos dance on the overhead plasma screens and the HUB SMART environment screensaver channel for the HUB is playing on the touchscreens below. The technobeam lights are projecting the Nortel phrase "How the world shares ideas" slowly on the floor below. This shot should is a static lock-down of 15 seconds (450 frames) and LOOPABLE. It is understood that not all of the kiosks will be viewable from this angle. From just inside the HUB, a SLOW dolly shot from the rightmost HUB kiosk station left towards the INFONODE. The framing of this shot would include the bottom of the kiosk stations (just below the touchscreens) up to the top of the plasma. A wide-angle lens might be needed from 3DSM. For timing, the shot should travel the length of the 5 kiosk stations during 12 seconds (360 frames). Close up shot of touchscreen with HUB screensaver channel animation playing. The shot should frame up to show mainly the entire touchscreen with a bit of space around the edges. This should be a static lock-down shot. 7 seconds of this shot should do (210 frames). Same as SHOT 3, but without the HUB screensaver channel. An alpha channel "hole" where the screen is will allow us to layer in other interface screens here. A still frame of

	this will do (1 frame).
	Medium shot of the plasma screen overhead with a crane up to reveal the sound dome mounted about. The majority of the kiosk station should be seen from just below the plasma up to the top of the plasma. The crane up will probably have to dolly back as well so that the Sound Dome will not eat the frame – it needs to be visible. 7 seconds of this shot should do (210 frames).
Narration: The InfoNode is an intelligent, web-browser driven environment. It provides you with a media-rich, easily accessible database of Nortel Networks' applications featured in the Center. The InfoNode represents the dynamic, high-bandwidth environment that Nortel Networks delivers.	A slow dolly into the space from just outside of the HUB (through the first door into the INFONODE). The camera should creep in and move to the right as it pans past the kiosk stations. On the 17" monitors is the INFONODE screensaver channel animation. This shot should last 12 seconds (360 frames).
	Close up shot of 17" monitor with INFONODE screensaver channel animation playing. The shot should frame up to show mainly the entire screen with a bit of space around the edges. This should be a static lock-down shot. 7 seconds of this shot should do (210 frames).
By clicking on Add to My Site, any information you wish to have available for future reference can be automatically stored on your personal web space at www.nortelguest.com. You may preview your personal web space by clicking on the "My Site" icon at any time.	Video shot of someone clicking on add to my site and then clicking on My Site to view his personal web page.
	Same as SHOT 2, but without the INFONODE screensaver channel. An alpha channel "hole" where the screen is will allow us to layer in other interface screens here. A still frame of this will do (1 frame).
	Static shot from high up looking down on the south end of the INFONODE. The 17" monitors should show the INFONODE screensaver channel animation. 7 seconds of this shot should do (210 frames).
Narration In the SimSpace, five custom kiosks stations are provided for you to interact with rich multimedia content. Application simulations entertainingly demonstrate the power of Nortel Networks' solution sets featured in the Center	This is an angle up shot from the walkway in SIMSPACE looking up at the kiosk stations. Once again, a wide-angle lens in 3DSM will most likely be necessary to get any type of shot here. This is a slow dolly shot which should take 12 seconds to go from the first kiosk station to the fourth one (360 frames).
	Close up shot of a 21" monitor with SIMSPACE screensaver channel animation playing. The shot should frame up to show mainly the entire screen with a bit of space around the edges.

	This should be a static lock-down shot. 7 seconds of this shot should do (210 frames).
	Same as SHOT 2, but without the SIMSPACE screensaver channel. An alpha channel "hole" where the screen is will allow us to layer in other interface screens here. A still frame of this will do (1 frame).
	Static view of one kiosk station framed as wide as possible to get the most of the millwork and technology. A still frame of this will do (1 frame).
Narration The FutureNow is a dramatic space built with a stereoscopic projector and a 50-inch plasma display. This area is used for demonstrating prototypes and concepts. High-level flexibility and unique media deliverables will provide you with a hands-on experience in a virtual environment.	This is a slow dolly shot inside of the FUTURENOW zone. The shot should start from the center of the room towards the BARON light table. A VR animation is playing on the unit. The shot should stop with the BARON almost full in the frame – 7 seconds total (210 frames).
The Network Challenge will playfully test your knowledge of Nortel Networks' solutions that you have experienced throughout the Center.	This is the same as SHOT 1 except pointing in the opposite direction – this time towards the 50" plasma. The network game interface is on the plasma monitor. Total time of shot should be 7 seconds total (210 frames).
	Close up of BARON screen. An alpha channel "hole" where the screen is will allow us to layer in other interface screens here. A still frame of this will do (1 frame).
	Close up of 50" plasma screen. An alpha channel "hole" where the screen is will allow us to layer in other interface screens here. A still frame of this will do (1 frame).
Narration: We hope you enjoy your experience at Nortel Networks Executive Briefing Center and discover the many ways in which the world shares ideas.	Fast paced shot sequence of space evolving into the logo (animated)
	FADE TO BLACK.

Chapter 7: Vignette CBC
We weren't quite Pixar, but we gave it our best shot

As web technologies were developing rapidly in the late 1990's so were software tools for the video producer. One emerging tool was an animation program called Poser. Poser aided in the creation of animated, 3D people. The animator could choose from a library of characters, adjust their postures and create moving 3D models that could then be placed into a virtual environment. There were two 3D animators that I worked with regularly, on using LightWave 3D and the other using 3D Studio Max. Between the two, we had a powerful team that could create about anything we could dream up. The only problem was time, money, and processing power. We always pushed the edge of our machine capabilities, but in 3D development, we always came down to the wire. A project for a new client gave us the opportunity to put these new tools to work.

Vignette was a company based in Dallas that focused on web software. They were a pioneer in Content Management Software or CMS. Their products allowed a company like a car dealership to use a set of web development tools to create costumer focused website, allowing members to create profiles, manage their interests, share their comments about a purchase, and interact with others in the community. Today this type of web site is very common, but in the late nineties this was extremely cutting edge. It bridged the web with CRM or customer relationship management, a concept that we had exploited with the design of Destination Nortel Networks.

Like many of our clients, Vignette had a customer briefing center at their headquarters. This CBC consisted of a small lobby and a few conference rooms where potential clients would be introduced to the company and its solutions. This is where a large amount of business was generated, and Vignette wanted to add the "Wow" factor that VisionFactory was becoming known for to this space. The plan was to create a hi-tech lobby which included a number of interactive kiosks with entertaining product demos and a "theater piece" that would be shown on the conference room screen. Like other CBC work we had done, the plan included a customer experience design that managed the flow of the visit, increasingly allowing the visitor to learn about the company's offerings as the sales team lead them into the pitch meeting. For Vignette, it was very important show how cutting edge the firm was, so the kiosk designs were sleek and a looping animation was also created for a group of configurable LCD screens that could be seen through the lobby glass.

The pitch to Vignette was to create something we had never tried – a 3D animated story with human characters. We decided on a motif we had done successfully before, a boardroom setting with interactions between different executives of a company discussing the value to the client's product. This allowed us to limit the action of our human renderings and make the challenge a little more manageable. The other godsend was finding a plug-in for the Poser software that was able to synch lip movements of the characters based on the recorded sound files. We knew that we could record the dialog, edit the flow and then work our animation timing from that audio track.

This video was by far the most complex technological challenge we had taken on. The building, conference room, furnishings, and characters all had to be created and customized. Their movements had to be orchestrated to seem as realistic as possible, and the dialogue had to play as if this was a regular movie, complete with continuity editing, shot selection, close ups and reaction shots. This meant that despite all of the technology involved, the scripting part of the process was actually pretty straight forward. We had a number of product details we needed to highlight, and we could take this askew way of telling the story to plug them in. Our tongue-in-cheek corporate boardroom would hopefully be an entertaining experience to introduce these new web concepts to potential clients.

Now, you would think our attempt to be a mini corporate Pixar would have been complex enough, but we decided to take our challenge a couple of steps further. Vignette wanted the interactive kiosks in the CBC lobby to be an area where customers could pick and choose demos of their web platform used for different industries. To accomplish this, we created interactive "Agents" from our animated characters. We had previously used Microsoft's Agent development kit for a Nortel project and we knew that we could render a number of actions and program in an on-demand interactive way. Agent is familiar to most people as the program that powered the MS Word paperclip and a number of other annoying help characters. By using this engine, we could create a web demo with our 3D characters popping up over the page now then and delivering marketing messaging. The amount of coordination in the programming and development of these elements was a little like playing 3D chess, but the team loved it, knowing it was something no one had ever tried before.

Scripting for these kiosk elements included mapping the menu choices and creating sequences for each possibility. This was "choose your own adventure" – corporate style. For most of the interactive scripts I had written, the process was always very intuitive. There wasn't a great resource on structure or how to plan something like this. Mostly the process involved outlining the number of interactions we had discussed with the client, trying to make them as entertaining and informative as possible, and perhaps most importantly, trying to keep them short. There was always an attempt to cram too much information into narration, and fighting back against that could mean the difference between making the user smile or boring them to death.

The Vignette project was a big deal for our company for many reasons. It really helped us branch out in new technologies, pushing our creative team and establishing our presence with a new influential client. It became a nice showcase for our work, where it would be seen by many other potential clients. It also established our credibility in working with another emerging web tech company. But in one way, the project was an ominous peak for the company. Projects like this, ones that had generous budgets from companies competing for their share of the boom in dotcom investing, would soon grow more and more scarce. Companies like Nortel, HP, Cisco, and smaller startups like Vignette, would all be impacted by the coming bust in tech investment. As we would find in the coming years, the first thing to go when companies started to tighten their belts was the pie in the sky marketing budgets. It was good while it lasted, and the Vignette project was a great one to create on someone else's dime.

Following are a variety of production documents and the Vignette script.

Through digital storytelling, Vignette success stories will come to life. As a framework for EBC experience, VisionFactory will create an interactive storyline that the visitor will encounter in three phases – pre-visit, onsite, and post-visit. This storyline will follow the upper management of a fictitious company looking to solve many pressing issues involving their E-business strategies. Story points take place at several "virtual locations" and are viewed at two specific locations – the visitor's browser (home or office etc.) and the EBC demo space. In addition there is a reference to the visitor's character on the Palm Device that is given to him at the beginning of the visit, and there is a final reference involving the character in to the closing visit mosaic.

This storytelling framework is designed to be scalable and modular providing the opportunities to add future demos and to easily port into other presentation formats such as CD-ROM and content packets for the online sales tool.

Each script follows one of five characters through the entire story. Through each character's story, we will initially explore the following Vignette solutions:

- Brix 2 Clix
- RMS
- On Display
- V5 Architecture
- Vignette Solutions Overview (suitable for any visitor)

The characters and storyline will:

- Illuminate the pressing needs of the fictitious company
- Learn about a specific Vignette Solution
- Interact with the demos, highlighting the benefits to the company
- Summarize in a report-back to the CEO character the high level marketing points of the Vignette solution
- Provide humor while educating about Vignette
- Introduce personalization to the visitor's experience
- Provide "wow" factor via storytelling and animation techniques

Treatment

The story begins with the CEO of our company being interviewed on the "We Mean Business" television program. He is lauded for his great success and reminisces about how the company developed its e-strategies.

In flashback during a boardroom meeting, we are introduced to the top four executives of the company, each facing a challenge that only Vignette solutions can solve. The CEO assigns each executive his or her mission. For instance CTO Nathan Catfive is tasked to find a scalable, reliable server architecture that leverages the company's existing platform and investment. Knowing deep down that he has a challenge in front of him, Catfive confidently assures the CEO that it will be no problem.

Later at his son's soccer game, Catfive has an epiphany as he is struck on the head by a ball – remembering a review of the V5 Architecture from Vignette. He decides at that moment to book a flight to Austin. The other executives including the VP of Marketing and Director of Publishing have similar epiphany moments, after which they all decide to explore Vignette.

Following their character to the briefing center, the EBC visitors share their experience. Once onsite the visitor interacts with Vignette demonstrations and the character provides feedback from the company perspective. For instance, while the V5 Architecture demo explains the many components of hardware and software, Nathan Catfive highlights how this benefits the company's bottom line. This interaction of technical demo and storytelling allows the visitors to more easily identify with the impact of the Vignette solution to their own company. Once the Demo is completed, the character reports back to the CEO giving a quick wrap-up of the why they should partner with Vignette. The story concludes back in the "We Mean Business" studio with the CEO summarizing how Vignette was a critical component to their success.

Name: Johnny Slingshot

Job Title: VP of Sales

Department: eCommerce

Mission: brix to clix

Lifestyle Description: Single, hip, loves frappacino mocha latte half skim

Gadget: Super-Duper PDA

On Vignette: "I chose Vignette because of their reputation, expertise and ability to provide all of the solutions to our business challenges."

Name: Nathan Catfive

Job Title: CTO

Department: Systems

Mission: V5 Architecture/ CMS (OVERVIEW VIGNETTE OFFERING)

Lifestyle Description: Soccer Dad, techno geek

Gadget: Sports Watchie Talkie

On Vignette: "Vignette provides a great architectural foundation for managing a complex and successful ebusiness application."

Name: Wendy Whipper-Snapper

Job Title: VP of Marketing

Department: Customer self service

Mission: RMS- Wendy needed a more scalable and cost-effective solution to accommodate the company's dramatic growth and customer demand.

Lifestyle Description: Mother of 3, practices kick boxing and yoga

Gadget: Cyber-One Card – calling card, library card, credit card, Driver's License - all in one

On Vignette: "We are always a few steps ahead of our competitors because of Vignette."

Name: Terri Topnotch

Job Title: Systems Engineer

Department: Portal

Mission: On-Display

Lifestyle Description: Loves gourmet cooking

Gadget: Cyber Cell Phone

> ***On Vignette:*** *"Thanks to Vignette, our team has harnessed the power of the Internet."*

Fade In:

Corporate Promotional Video for UNITED MOTOR CORPORATION

Music pipes up – energetic and corporate. Cheese factor is there, but not too much. Narrator is a little cheesier, bold and commanding.

Celebrating 75 years of service, quality and innovation, United Motor Corporation takes you into the 21st Century with new ways of serving the customer. Bold new connectivity. New ways to purchase and deliver. Online, just in time. UMC leads the way in Internet commerce from the national level, to each dealer. Easy to employ, update, integrate and promulgate. UMC, the automobiles of the Information Super Highway.

The UMC logo animates on.

CUT FROM FLASH TO QT VIDEO:

INT. UMC CORPORATION HQ – EXECUTIVE BOARD ROOM

Inside this larger corporate boardroom, seated around the table are four of UMC's top executives.

CEO Webster Williams a mid-fifties businessman – confident, yet hip is speaking from the head of the room.. Behind him on the large screen is a UMC Corp logo. Camera moves slowly toward him across the table.

Webster

> So everyone. There is the vision. Online development, management, and rollout of our e-commerce strategy for the corporate level and for our affiliates and dealers. Now all we have to do is make it work. But It's not going to be an easy task. We must have an end-to-end solution, and we must take advantage of our existing investments.

Nathan Catfive, the CTO, is watching, with a worried look on his face. Slowly we move from medium to close up on Nathan's eyes – the look of terror as he thinks to himself.

                              CEO

        Catfive!?

Nathan is startled by the CEO.

                              Nathan

        Yes sir.

The CEO Turns to a whiteboard as he talks and scribbles a diagram at breakneck speed while
delivering his lines.

                              CEO

        You will be responsible for solving our platform dilemma. Something that leverages
        our investments to date, utilizes our existing skills base. A platform that's reliable,
        scalable and secure. Content management tools, and support for our other initiatives.

        Got it?

Back on Nathan looking toward CEO.

                              Nathan

        No problem, sir.

Webster turns to a woman on the other side of the table.

                              CEO

        Good. Wendy, we've got to work on our customer relationships and marketing strategies.
        Better data mining. We need targeted messages across multiple touch points. Wireless, web,
        everywhere.

                              Wendy

You got it boss.

                               CEO

Slingshot.

                    Johnny Slingshot (energetic)

Yes sir!

                               CEO

Johnny, it's your job to make our e-commerce strategy a reality. I want easy to use and
mange online dealerships for us and our clients. Remember it has to be secure and handle any
level of traffic. Let's not screw up like we did before.

                    Johnny Slingshot (humble)

Yes sir.

                               CEO

And Terri. Shore up our B2B communications. This is critical to the company. We need
seamless and reliable ways to talk to our partners, customers, even our competitors. The
network has to work for the business.

                               Terri

I'm on the case sir.

CEO recaps the missions as we cut reactions to CEO.

                               CEO

Excellent. Now let's recap our requirements. Slingshot, you're responsible for getting our e-
commerce engine functioning, not just for us, but for our clients. Whipper-Snapper, we need
more effective data mining and better customer communication across multiple touch points.
Topnotch, shore up our B2B backend – a bulletproof software solution, and Catfive, you're

going select a platform that pulls all of this together. Okay? Thanks everybody. Be careful out there.

INT. VIGNETTE LOBBY – DAY

Our four UMC employees stand in the lobby taking in the welcome mosaic. Close up on one monitor shows an animation and the words "Welcome UMC Corporation"

Scene 15 *(Character-specific)*

(This sequence is displayed on the demo pod screen in the Vignette Demo Space.)

INT. VIGNETTE DEMO SPACE – DAY

Nathan is standing by a demo pod.

Nathan

Let's see what they've got.

AT THIS POINT NATHAN DISAPPEARS FROM THE VIDEO IN A STAR TREK LIKE BEAMING SEQUENCE. THEN THE VIDEO WINDOW CLOSES.

The Page changes to the splash screen of the Overview V5/CMS Demo. Nathan then reappears over this screen with a "beam on" transition. He now rides onto of the existing screen.

Nathan

Hey. You know I came here to look at the V5 Architecture, but it looks like there's a lot more I can learn about. I might need your help. Where should we start?

At this point a menu system of navigation choices appears. The visitor must choose the item.

(Demo Series)

The pattern is demonstration material section followed by Nathan restating the top benefits to his company. This allows the demonstration to play out in any fashion and Nathan will always respond with the high-level marketing points for his company.

Scene 17 *(Character-specific)*

INT. VIGNETTE DEMO SPACE – DAY

Nathan addresses his "Video Watch Phone" to report back to the UMC CEO. CU on Watch phone shows CEO.

Nathan

Good news, Chief. Vignette's RMS and V5 Architecture are perfect for our goals. It's open, scalable, reliable and secure, plus it supports all of the services we've talked about. We've found our platform.

CEO

Good work. I think we've got ourselves a new partner. Talk to you later. I've got another call.

….next 3 report outs.

Fade out.

Chapter 8: Sun IFCBC
Another take on the Customer Briefing Center

Pitching Briefing Center work became a niche for VisionFactory. In fact, the act of pitching became a product in itself. Based on the success of our Nortel work and other Briefing Center jobs, we began to attract the attention of other corporate briefing center managers. Often a center looking to do a major redesign would hire us to create a media package and conceptual pitch. Sun Microsystems had an older center at its Santa Clara, California headquarters that they were looking to upgrade. We took a team to Silicon Valley and spent several days brainstorming with their team to re-imagine the customer space.

Sun's philosophy was that "the network is the computer", an idea that computer terminals didn't require huge amounts of processing speed and storage. Rather, a centralized supercomputer with many networked dumb terminals was a much more effect arrangement. This philosophy was quite different from the directions of PC's and Macs, but in a way more aligned with the emerging interconnectivity of the internet. Sun also was the home of Java, the ubiquitous language of choice for cross-platform programmers. The company was very successful and we saw the potential to work with them to create another great Briefing Center project.

Our ideas once again were a blend of architect and technology. We wanted to create a living space that felt like a destination and served as a metaphor of the company's offerings. The showcase piece of our piece was to be an animated walkthrough of the proposed space, showing the flow and the detailed ways in which the Sun technology would be presented. It would allow the client to experience our ideas long before they were built.

As with many of our big pitches, it turned out that Sun didn't eventually go with the ideas. But the vision of what would have been an exciting piece is still here. The surviving documents from the script show an evolution of how this script was written, first in a treatment form, then in Hollywood script format and finally in a two column format. The two column script was written concurrent with the creation of the space visualizations, so this example is much more visual.

Pre-Visit/Sales Confirmation Call:

The Journey

Hi, my name is Will Mathers, CIO of Exentis Technologies in Boise. Six months ago our business decided to explore how to offer our new financial applications over the Web. I was familiar with Sun, having seen them at several technology trade shows. Since we needed hardware, software, and expertise beyond our internal resources, we decided to see what Sun could offer to jumpstart our proposed ASP model.

After initial conversations with a local Sun representative, we were encouraged to visit the new iForce Customer Briefing Center in Silicon Valley. I had heard through the grapevine that it was a very cool space, but I had no idea before visiting that it would leapfrog our ASP strategy light years forward.

Net Ready

Before my departure to Menlo Park, I received an email inviting me to visit a web site for a pre-visit message. Up popped a video animation sequence, personalized with my name and company information, that piqued my interest. It explained that the iFCBC was both collaborative meeting space and a place where I could explore the possibilities on my own. It also provided me with the opportunity to correct any inaccuracies in my customer profile. It even had links to travel accommodations, local points of interest, and other potentially useful resources. I was able to provide feedback to the CBC staff about meal preferences and tell them what we hoped to achieve at the meeting. Needless to say, this really helped me prepare for the trip, and I made sure our CEO Frank and the other Exentis representatives took advantage of this resource.

Meeting Day

We arrived in Menlo Park on a Sunday evening and settled into our hotel. Just before heading to Sun on Monday morning, we discussed how to get the most out of the day. We agreed to keep the dialogue focused on issues surrounding technical deployment strategy. We wanted to see a mix of products and solutions, but we also we wanted to get an overall vision from the company. And being a CIO, I hoped to cover some of the financial and business factors as well. I didn't know how customized the visit would be.

I was in for a great surprise.

Arrival

As we approached the Menlo Park campus my anticipation grew. We walked from the car into the covered entry to Building 15 where the music and the décor were a nice change of pace from the 101 traffic.

In the lobby we were greeted by the receptionist and welcomed to the iForce Customer Briefing Center. I was struck by design of the space. Integrated into the reception desk was a series of interesting interactive stations that featured Sun LCD screens and a tiny high-tech cameras. Across the room to the right, there was this mysterious tunnel made of steel and glass which seemed gloww on the inside. I had seen some of this on the website, but I was much more impressed standing in the space.

The receptionist pointed out the screens above the elevators and explained that our group information including agenda and meeting room location would always be available. There were also a series of Sun animations on an adjacent screen. By coincidence or design, just as I looked up the animation spelled out, "The Sun iForce CBC welcomes Exentis Corporation" and the Sun and Exentis logos flew onscreen. This even got a smile out of our CEO Frank.

Guiding us to the interactive stations, the receptionist explained that we would each be given a photo smart card that would serve as our passport to all of the features of the briefing center. She had us each step up to one of the stations and confirm our name, company and position and told us how the smart card would allow us to view and save personalized product and solution information to our personal website. I glanced up at the sign over the lobby. "The network is the computer," it read. I started to get an idea of what they were talking about.

We confirmed a couple of items on the screens, and the receptionist had each of us face the camera, smile and -SNAP- took our pictures. We were even given a choice of what picture to use for our badges. Then, while our cards were being printed, the receptionist showed us a two minute introduction to the iForce CBC. This presentation explained that we were about to experience a showcase of Sun's vision, products, solutions and services. It touched on the philosophy of the iForce concept and stressed that Sun is the trusted advisor in the internet economy. Then it prepared us for the next step. What was on the other side of that tunnel?

We were given our badges and Brian, our sales rep., guided us toward the tunnel.

Transition Tunnel

Our group approached what appeared to be a tunnel lined with fiber optics. As we entered the tunnel, streams of data packets danced from one end of the tunnel to the other. As this happened around me, I realized that I was inside the Internet - a moving packet of data pushing my way into another place. I sensed that our movements caused the effects to change and respond.

I could faintly detect the sounds of people speaking. I could hear Scott McNeely saying "...as we've stated over and over, the network is the computer and today's market indicates we were right." Another voice saying, "...welcome Exentis Technologies to the Sun iForce Customer Briefing Center." Through the end of the tunnel, I could see an intriguing blend of computer lab space and unique curved glass rooms. I felt like we were entering a different world. Frank smiled even more here. Frank doesn't normally smile.

iForce Space

Brian walked us through the open presentation area, a mix equipment and unique spaces for collaboration and presentation. It felt like I had stepped onto a Star Trek movie set, only one where they were planning to build a better Enterprise (no pun intended). Brian informed us that we would be seeing the iForce lab in action throughout in the day, but first we'd settle into our conference room.

Conference Room

Our executives at Exentis pride themselves on having nicely appointed meeting facilities, but our conference room at the iFCBC was something else. It featured integrated audio and video conferencing, laptop connections in the table, and crisp, bright data projection for the presentation material. The room itself had a comfortable, relaxing atmosphere, comfy chairs, soft lighting, and excellent coffee!

When we got down to discussing our network configuration, one of the coolest features became apparent. Integrated into the room walls were white board areas that could be revealed when needed. The sale representative asked if he could digitally capture this part of the session for his information, and we approved. Interestingly enough, a small camera and embedded microphone picked up the session and recorded it to an MPEG2 file! We were informed we could take a DVD copy of the session home with us (or stream the session to our personal web space). After we hashed out some of our networking needs, Brian told us it was time for an iForce tour.

The iForce Primer

Just then the lights dimmed, and an animated video began playing. The video was comprised of a 3D model of the iForce space. By flying from one point to another the video explained each area and its focus. This wasn't some trade show booth, this felt more like a journey. The iForce lab, Solution Set Area, Storage, Netra, Servers, DotCom Home, Partnering, after seeing this we realized that Sun had much more to offer us than we first imagined.

Before beginning our tour, Brian gave us a ten minute break, so I walked around the area outside of our conference room and tried out my smart card in one of the Sun Ray terminals. Right as I inserted the card my personal mysun.sun home page appeared. In addition to the other useful information, there was now an integrated menu for my iForce CBC visit. During the short break I was able to bookmark three Sun "Heroes Program" features and watch that new funny Sun commercial streaming from an MPEG-2 Server. Maybe these are some features we'll be able to offer our customers, I thought.

Orientation Area

After our break Brian led us to one of the impressive glass "silos" in the main iForce space. As Brian pressed something on the Palm device he was carrying, I noticed that above the entrance the LED ticker display read "Exentis Technologies".

This glass enclosed oval room had piqued my interest before, but it was even more interesting inside. Incorporated into the space were three equipment racks full of Sun boxes and flat panel displays. These racks also connected to other parts of the iForce space in a sort of virtual network layout. While we were filing in, our CTO Nathan Catfive leaned over to me and smiled saying, "The Network is the computer." I nodded in agreement.

Our group leaned against a rail while Brian introduced a gentleman from the iForce team. He explained the history of Sun's iForce philosophy and touched a screen on his podium to launch a three screen presentation entitled "Vision and Value". The coolest thing about the presentation was the way it was projected onto three different panes of the Glass room. Also it was interesting to be in an enclosed area with our group, but still feel part of a larger, active space. After the brief introduction ended, the iForce rep. told us about the current Proof of Concept that was taking place in the iForce Lab. He was able to use his podium to control a variety of graphics and animations to explain how Sun and XYZ Corporation were performing an interoperability exercise with the newest fiber switching technologies. With confidence he stated, "This is where we have breakthroughs every day that affect the way people do business."

Solution Set Area

Next the iForce rep. took us to an area featuring Sun solution sets. This area included a presentation area and several industry specific kiosks that featured solution set overviews. We were shown a media presentation of a Sun solution applicable to the financial marketplace. Then we discussed our upcoming challenges. It was good to see that past successes were documented. This gave our team a sense that Sun understood what we were up against.

Before leaving this area Brian encouraged us to revisit this space and explore some of the case studies later during our break.

Proof of Concept Lab

Next we walked to the Proof of Concept lab where we were shown a diagram of the current POC project. The iForce rep. explained how Sun and XYZ were utilizing the featured equipment in the racks to simulate the actual network configuration the company was proposing. Inside the lab area we could see XYZ and Sun engineers working side-by-side. The white boards and monitors were filled with interesting data and activity. Immediately I thought that we would be a prime candidate for a similar Proof of Concept and mentioned this to Brian. He told me that we should examine this further and that we may even become a candidate to host an iForce-ready center in the future.

Lunchtime

After spending some time examining the lab area, Brian guided us back to the conference room and then to lunch. He explained that after lunch there would be a break during which we were welcome to explore the center and interact with any of the customer experience stations. These Sun stations were located in various parts of the space and featured contextual information. They could also be used to access our personal web spaces to bookmark particular media, documents and other materials.

After a comfortable lunch in a very nice dining area I broke from the group to make a phone call. I entered a futuristic looking chamber where I could use the phone, check my email, and surf the web.

Kiosks and passive media

Next, I walked around the iForce area and explored different self-serve demonstration kiosks. Some featured particular hardware in the racks, and others focused on a variety of solution sets. Even though there were other groups in the space, I still could explore information at my own pace at these stations. Planning to share the info when I returned to Exentis, I loved being able to insert my smart card into any of these machines and bookmark certain presentations on my personal website.

Before returning to the conference room, I stopped to watch a presentation looping on one of the two large video walls integrated in the equipment racks. This particular presentation was dedicated to the history of innovation within Sun.

The Afternoon

Reconvening in the conference room, our group began to focus on ideas about building our ASP infrastructure. A question on server requirements prompted Brian to contact an iForce engineer in an adjacent building via a streaming video link. We were able to get expert advice instantly from the same engineer that was later going to give us an overview of Sun's line of Servers. Questions about Storage solutions led Brian to schedule an overview in the storage area later in the afternoon. Brian also explained that the racks within the iForce area featured several integrated demonstrations of Sun solutions as well as individual product demos. In addition, he mentioned that all of the media technology and software were driven by Sun hardware. "We believe in walking the walk," he said.

Demonstration Space

We had a sort of whirlwind tour of Sun products during the afternoon. This included a multi-media and hardware presentation in the Storage Area and an overview of several server configurations. We also took a look at the Netra line in another area, where we saw an interactive presentation about decreased footprint, reliability and redundancy. All of this helped to address our business concerns.

During these presentations, everyone in the group was thrilled by the clever way the room was set up. The series of racks really helped us visualize our own network and how all of the pieces would fit together.

Partner Corner

Next Brian explained that the partnering area of the Center was a showcase for those companies that have "bet" on Sun and have had tremendous success through integrated partnerships.   The room was filled with a combination of fixtures, screens and some printed material. It looked like a mini trade show booth.

One of our vendors, Oracle, was the featured partner in the space. As we walked through their exhibit we saw how, by using Sun solutions, Oracle and a variety of other partners were able to offer the fastest, most reliable platforms to many top ASP's, some of which were our competitors.   Brian showed us an overview video about the partnership which featured commentary by Scott McNealy, and Oracle's CEO. We also were able to select and view different network diagrams of Sun/Oracle solutions and surf through testimonials from third party participants on the Sun workstations within the space.

DotCom Home
As the last stop during our journey, the DotCom Home was touted as a combination of Sun innovation and partnership showcase dedicated to the network connected home. I wasn't sure what to expect although I had peeked into the space earlier in the day. Brian guided us to the entrance of the area, and we first saw a media-based introduction to the space.   The presentation pointed out Sun's continual dedication to innovative technologies and the many partners that look to Sun as a trusted advisor.

As we moved into the space I was struck by the futuristic notions of the networked home but Brian pointed out how all of the technologies and products showcased are readily available. He also emphasized how Sun's core technologies were the common thread between all of these products. I looked around - Sony, Panasonic, Ford, Whirlpool, Frigidare - these were significant allies. I have to admit, though this space didn't apply directly to Exentis's immediate plans, it did make me think about Sun in yet another way. Frank loved the idea of a networked curling iron.

Wrapping it up
At the end of our day I felt that this was the perfect way to learn about Sun. Not only did I understand the company's philosophy, I got the sense they understood our company and the challenges we faced. We really do need a trusted advisor in the networked economy, and I'm convinced Sun will be it.

As Brian led us back through the iForce space and out through the tunnel, I began planning my next trip to the center. Who should I bring this time?
I can't wait to see what's new.

Music pipes up. It's a whimsical techie beat.

Sun purple LED ticker style lettering scrolls onto the black screen accompanied by beeping sound fx:

    "The Sun files:"

Below another line in red scrolls on:

    "Exentis Technologies"

A third red line scrolls on just below, as the top one scrolls off:

    "Chief Information officer – Will Mathers"

These two ticker lines remain onscreen as computer window opens onto the screen. Within the window is the image of a young business executive. He stands in a corporate lobby with a large Exentis logo on the wall. Though he's not moving, the camera pushes in slowly toward him.

               Will Mathers (vo)
      That's me. Here at Exentis I'm the new kid on the block.
      Three months in and I'm already responsible for a new series of
      online financial services. We're launching a new ASP model,
      and it's my responsibility to make sure we've chosen the best
      partners to make it happen. That's why I first suggested Sun.

The title tickers scroll of the screen and the "window" expands to full screen animation.

Int. Exentis Technologies – Will Mather's Desk – Day

Will is seated in front of his computer. The camera moves slowly from behind him, over his shoulder toward his computer screen, a Sun LCD screen. Onscreen Will is looking at a Sun web page about the iForce CBC.

               Will
      I talked to Brian, our Sun account manager, about our plans, and
      he suggested that a team from Exentis come to see the new
      iForce Customer Briefing Center in Menlo Park. We set up a
      visit and Brian pointed me to a customized web site to get started.

The camera is now tighter on the screen. The site features information about the center. Will clicks a couple of items. A video plays in one window.

               Will
      The site was great. I learned the latest developments at Sun,
      plus there was information to help me plan the trip. I was able
      to give feedback to the center's staff, and I got a peek at some of the
      new features we would be seeing. Based on everything I knew about

the company, I thought our visit to Sun would be a big step forward.

The computer screen nearly fills the frame now. Fade out.

A ticker title scrolls on:

> "Arrival"

> and scrolls off.

Fade in:

Ext. sun iFCBC – Morning

The doors to the iFCBC lobby open, and the camera moves between them. Inside the lobby are three people standing. A tunnel entrance to the iForce area can be seen across the room, as can the quote "The network is the computer". The receptionist desk takes the focus.

> Will
> This was my first trip to Sun so I didn't know what to expect.
> As we entered lobby, the receptionist welcomed us and
> guided us to a series of registration stations. She explained
> that we'd each be given a personalized smart card to use
> throughout the day. In addition to being our Sun security badge,
> these cards could be used to access our personal web sites on any
> of the terminals in the center. And our pictures made the badges
> a personal takeaway from the visit.

Series of shots:
- Camera moves to the registration stations
- CU on one station
- Onscreen there is the message "Welcome Exentis Technologies" and a rotating Sun iForce Smartcard is animated on the screen.
- Wide – from behind three of the visiting team at the terminals- three hanging plasmas over the elevators can be seen.

> Will
> The receptionist pointed out the lobby information screens that
> told us which conference room we'd be using. Then our rep Brian
> joined the group and led us into the center.

The camera moves through the tunnel and into the iForce area. The landscape is revealed and the camera cuts (or turns) to Will who stands before the tunnel.

> Will
> As we moved through the tunnel, I noticed the lights and sounds
> responded to our movement. At this point I realized we were
> in for an interesting day. Entering the space, Brian explained that
> the new design was about showcasing Sun solutions. The products
> and demonstrations were there for us to "kick the tires" and to see
> entire systems in action.

We now move through the space. There is media and "tickers" showing different activity. The closest video wall displays a Sun logo and a message "Welcome Exentis Technologies".

Camera passed by kiosks, racks, and a large glass oval room. The ticker there says "Sun Solution Sets".
Another ticker reads, "Now showing – Telco Solutions from Netra"

> Will
> Brian also pointed out the Proof of Concept Area and
> explained we'd learn more about the work in progress there.

Int. iFCBC Conference Room – Day

Camera starts on the screen at the end of the conference room and slowly pulls back to reveal the room. There
are whiteboards on either side of the table. Several people are seated. A couple of laptops are on the table.
Brian stands behind a podium.

> Will
> In the conference room Brian introduced us to
> the concept behind the iForce CBC, and collaborated
> on some our ideas for new financial services.
> This room was great. The connectivity and
> whiteboards were very convenient, and when we had a question about
> servers, Brian was able to pull up a video connection with an iForce
> engineer for instant feedback. We even captured part
> of our brainstorming session on digital video.

Series, gliding, maybe dissolves:
- Screen shows Sun Presentation (including images of iForce space)
- Show network diagram on whiteboard
- Show laptop on table connected
- Possibly a couple of Sun Rays incorporated in the table
- Show video of Engineer on the screen
- Push in to a LCD screen with a wide shot of the room mapped into a window (SME-C-R)

Dissolve to:

Int. iFCBC Hallway – Day

The hallway just outside of the conference room leads to a breakout area with a few chairs and a few Sun Ray
terminals. The camera moves down this hall toward Will, now standing. He is looking at one of the all-in-one
Sun Ray machines.

> Will
> During a break I tried out my smart card in
> one of the new Sun Rays outside of the conference room.

Close up of the Card inserted into the machine. Onscreen is Will's personal Web Site. Elements include:
- Getting the most from you iForce CBC visit (including a simple diagram of the iForce space)
- 5 .com Heroes Thumbnails with text
- Sun Storage Solutions
- Featured Partner – Oracle

The Page is simple and easy to understand.

> Will
> Not only did my personal desktop pop up, but it included the
> type of information I was looking for. There was an interactive

map of the iForce area and multimedia pieces about Sun success
stories. I bookmarked two of these stories and sent another to
our network consultant back in Boise. I really like the concept
behind the Sun Ray, and was impressed by the customized
materials I could gather digitally.

Fade out.

Ticker scrolls on:

"iForce Ready Center"

...and scrolls off.

Fade in:

Int. iForce Area

The camera moves back through the hallway, by the phone stations toward the egg shaped glass rooms.
Above one of the rooms is a ticker sign. The ticker reads, "Welcome Exentis Technologies."

Int. Orientation "Egg"

The camera continues into the presentation space and settles at the back, facing the "screen" area. To the right
of the screens is a slick podium housing a flat panel control screen. To the right of that, along the wall are three
equipment racks full of Sun gear and three integrated monitors. A woman – the iForce Rep. stands behind the
podium.

    Will
  After our break, Brian led us to one of the presentation areas,
  where we were given an overview called "Vision and Values".
  The iForce representative navigated through a variety of videos and
  animations in this Immersive presentation. He was even able to
  respond to our questions using the media menu system at his podium. This
  experience was a great build-up for what was next.

This presentation is represented by three screens in the egg. The podium in an iNav interface which is shown in
close up. We need at least one point where the wide shot goes to iNav, something highlights, then medium shot
of the three screens responding to the input.

Int. Proof of Concept Area

The camera now approaches the POC. There is activity inside of the lab, and the iForce rep stands by a plasma
screen that cycles through some network diagrams. Inside are engineers standing by white boards.

    Will
  In the Proof of Concept area we saw an ongoing interoperability
  test being conducted by Sun and XYZ Corporation. While the
  engineers worked inside, we were shown how Sun servers and
  workstations were integrated with new fiber switches. Seeing an
  iForce POC in action, I mentioned to Brian that we'd be very
  interested in a similar exercise for our new service launch, and we
  agreed to begin planning the next steps to make it happen.

Dissolve to:

Int. Solution Set Area

The area is another presentation space. It includes a series of interaction stations branded by industry names. (see industry list in discovery doc.) The Racks in the area feature gear, integrated monitors, and two have large plasmas as well.

> Will
> Continuing our iForce tour, we visited the solution set area
> where a series of kiosks featured industry related media.
> And in the racks there were hardware demonstrations supporting
> past Proof of Concept successes.

Cut to:

Int. Solution Set "Egg"

Pulling back from a screen (projection onto the "egg" wall"), we see an animation from JCREW. The pull back reveals another three screen presentation – a spotlight on JCREW.

> Will
> Inside the presentation area we viewed a case study about
> Sun's leadership role in designing the architecture for jcrew.com.
> This session helped us address many of our own challenges and understand
> how Sun could help us.

The pull back continues. During the shot, onscreen there is a combination of video footage, network diagrams and bullets. It is an immersive display environment.

Fade out.

Fade in

Int. Dining Area

This a gliding shot down the dining space. Seated at one table are the group from Exentis and Sun reps.

> Will
> After a nice lunch, our group discussed strategies for our
> network infrastructure, and we were eager to take a look at some
> of the Sun Hardware showcased at the center.

Int. Demonstration Area

Wide shot that shows much of the rack "real estate" inside the space. The group stands around one area.

> Will
> In the afternoon, we toured the demonstration area,
> and I was beginning to understand how significant
> Sun's portfolio was.

Closer on the racks around the group. There are three large servers and some Sun Ray Stations in the rack. A small ticker Scrolls, "Server Solutions".

> ### Will
> In the storage and Netra areas we discussed two pressing
> issues of our network: scalability and reliability. The iForce staff 's
> expertise was just what we needed to work through these issues, and
> seeing the products working together was a big boost to our
> confidence.

Quick shots of the group at the Netra Space, and in the server areas. These may be closer angles in the existing presentation "silos". The gear in the racks reflects the Storage and Netra products.

Partnering Area

The camera starts on the outside of this area, where behind the glass, an exhibit about Oracle can be seen. There is ticker scrolling "Partner Pavilion featuring Oracle". Then it moves through the entrance and between exhibitry and media screens.

> ### Will
> After spending some time in the conference room,
> Brian said we should check out two more features of the
> center before leaving. First we toured the partnering
> space, where Sun's strategic partners displayed success
> stories resulting from their collaboration.

.com Home

Now the camera moves toward and into the .com home, passing a media presentation and gliding through the simulated apartment space. Integrated screens roll video or graphic content in each of the "rooms".

> ### Will
> And, our final stop was the .com home, a fascinating look
> at networked appliances, devices and services all based on Sun
> innovation and infrastructure. This area was both entertaining and
> informative, associating a variety of popular brand name
> manufacturers with Sun technologies.

Ticker title scrolls in:

> "Impressions"
> And scrolls off.

Series of clips from the day's experience. This is a wrap up montage/ recap.

> ### Will
> It was Sun's history and spirit of innovation that impressed
> everyone in our group. From the demonstrations, the iForce Lab,
> the Solutions Sets, .com home and partnerships, we'd seen an
> entire company's vision, through it's products, solutions and culture.
> I knew that everyone in my group now saw Sun in a new light.
> We needed an advisor and a partner as we moved forward. Thanks to
> This visit, I knew that advisor and partner would be Sun Microsystems.

Last recap image dissolves into Still of Sun logo. Holds on logo.

Fade out.

AUDIO	ANIMATION	NOTES

CHAPTER 1 - Pre-Visit Website

The new iForce Customer Briefing Center in Menlo Park combines the amenities of an executive briefing facility with the engineering elements of an iForce ready Center. The result is an exciting blend of Sun Solutions in an environment of collaboration and partnership.		
Customers are invited to the iFCBC to meet with Sun executives and iForce engineers and learn about the Net Effect, and SunONE, or Sun's Open Network Environment architecture.		
Before visiting the iForce Customer Briefing center, guests are pointed to a customized website containing the latest information about Sun and the features they will see at the center.		
This site also contains valuable information for their trip, including weather forecasts, restaurant recommendations and more. This channel of communication is the first stage of a customized experience for each visitor.		

CHAPTER 2:Lobby/Reception

Customers gather in the iFCBC lobby to collect their group and meet with their Sun sales representative. At the front desk, the receptionist welcomes visitors and guides them through the simple registration process. Customers can also use the concierge service to arrange later travel or dining plans.		

AUDIO	ANIMATION	NOTES
The receptionist provides guests with a personalized Smart Card to use throughout their iFCBC visit. Guests are told that the cards are multipurpose, functioning both as a security badge and the key to access their personal Sun web site at any of the kiosk terminals inside.		
The lobby also features digital signage displaying customer visit information and key Sun marketing imagery.		

CHAPTER 3 – The Portal

Leaving the lobby, guests walk through a dramatic hallway. This architectural element creates a metaphorical portal into the networked canvas of messaging and applications .		
The light filled portal serves as a transition into the showcase of products and solutions encompassing Sun's vision of the Net Effect.		
FX: montage of music, voices, swooshing/speeding sounds		
The portal opens to a striking vista of Sun solutions integrated into an engaging space, where the Open Network environment begins to take symbolic and physical shape before the visiting customers.		

CHAPTER 4 – Briefing Rooms

AUDIO	ANIMATION	NOTES
One of the key elements of the iFCBC is the impressive and functional conferencing space. The Briefing rooms feature an easy to use presentation platform that places a menu of multimedia elements at the fingertips of the sales force executives and iForce staff.		
In addition, videoconferencing and WebCam connectivity allow other parts of the iForce CBC, and other iForce centers throughout the world to become part of the conference room experience.		
Engineered for maximum flexibility and connectivity, the conference rooms exploit Sun hardware to create a unique collaborative environment.		

CHAPTER 5: Proof Of Concept

AUDIO	ANIMATION	NOTES
Customers come to the iFCBC not only to discuss Sun solutions, but also to see them in action. The Proof of Concept, or POC, space is a working lab where Sun engineers and customers work together on real world applications.		
At the heart of the iForce concept, the Proof Of Concept lab provides visitors with proof of Sun's dedication to partnership and innovation.		
The Proof Of Concept lab showcases Sun hardware and software applications in new ways, as the teams work through a variety of business challenges.		

AUDIO	ANIMATION	NOTES

CHAPTER 6: Solution Sets

AUDIO	ANIMATION	NOTES
Sun **Solution** Sets are showcased in an area that features a series of interactive kiosks and hardware supported demonstrations of past Proof of Concept successes.		
Including the presentation silos, the Solution Set space facilitates in-depth media supported presentations, as well as individually explored case studies.		
By pulling media presentations from a menu-driven, centralized database, all presentation areas within the center place a wealth of product and solution messaging at the fingertips of every presenter and visitor.		

CHAPTER 7: DEMONSTRATION

AUDIO	ANIMATION	NOTES
The iFCBC features a variety of demonstration areas complete with Sun hardware and software. Demonstrations can be given in the silos and, along the networked rack system throughout the center.		
Integrated presentation stations at key points provide a platform for both leader-led and user driven media experiences, and		

AUDIO	ANIMATION	NOTES
the networked rack systems provide a highly flexible forum for ever changing product and solution demonstrations including: Solaris, Sun Management Center, Wireless, Java, Jiro, Professional Services, High Performance computing, and more.		ALTERNATE READING: including: Solaris, Wireless, Java, Jiro, Professional Services, and more.

CHAPTER 8: Dining

AUDIO	ANIMATION	NOTES
Following a morning of business meetings, customers relax in the center's spacious, sun filled dining facility. The buffet style dining provides a pleasant setting for informal conversations.		
Within the dining area is the NewsBar. Here, multiple monitors play news broadcasts from around the world, to ensure guests can easily stay in touch with current market events.		
The open atmosphere of the Dining Area and NewsBar is both practical and pleasant, and continues to build upon the Sun ONE theme prevalent throughout the center.		

CHAPTER 9: Sun Ray Kiosks/Privacy Pods

AUDIO	ANIMATION	NOTES
During their center visit, customers are provided with areas for both private conversation and access to Sun information.		
The Privacy Pods feature a telephone, a Sun Ray, and laptop connectivity. These areas provide		

AUDIO	ANIMATION	NOTES
guests with the communication tools they need during their visit.		
Throughout the center, visitors can use their smart cards at Sun Ray kiosks to access their personalized mysun.com website and bookmark digital takeaways for later review. At these stations visitors can check on their agendas, navigate through interactive case studies, and view customer testimonial videos, and Sun Solutions information.		

CHAPTER 10: Partnering Area

Sun values its Partners' contributions. To strengthen key corporate relationships, the Sun iFCBC features the new Partnership Area.		
Set up as a mini-trade show exhibit, partner's Solution Set demonstration, or experiential media event, the partnership space showcases the vision of Sun partners and the value of betting on Sun solutions.		

CHAPTER 11: Connected Lifestyle

Entertaining and thought provoking, the Connected Lifestyle area presents a vision of the future, based on technologies readily available today.		
This area provides a fascinating look at networked appliances, devices and services based on Sun innovation and infrastructure.		
One of the most popular demonstration areas of the center, the Connected Lifestyle home illustrates Sun backed		

AUDIO	ANIMATION	NOTES
systems powering a variety of web enabled, innovative products. These are exhibited in collaboration with many high profile brand name manufacturers.		

CHAPTER 12: Conclusion

AUDIO	ANIMATION	NOTES
The iForce CBC is a testament to Sun Microsystem's history vision and strength. Here, customers see the Net Effect realized through Sun's products, solutions and culture.		
At the Sun iFCBC, each customer is treated as a unique guest. This center is the showcase of Sun solutions and engineering and makes a lasting impression on all who visit. Welcome to the future of the network.	iFCBC	
Welcome to the Sun iForce Customer Briefing Center	Sun microsystems We're the dot in .com	

Chapter 9: Arris
Is that an IMAX in your pocket?

The highest budgeted media piece we produced at VisionFactory was also one of the shortest. It was an all 3D animated video for Nortel and Antec called Arris. The concept was a 6-7 minute immersive animation describing a new technology that brought high speed internet based services into the home. The technology enabled many of the features of broadband networking that we've become accustomed to today such as ecommerce, video on demand, and video calling. Long before there was Skype, digital cable TV, ubiquitous DSL, and cable modems, the Arris project seemed like a distant futuristic vision. Nortel had partnered with the equipment manufacturer Antec hoping to be the supplier to cable networks looking for this amazing technology.

Since the market for this equipment was so huge, Nortel wanted to go all out on a production that would wow its audiences. The presentation was to be produced primarily for a single high profile tradeshow. Knowing we had to make a big impact not only with the media, but in the way it was presented, we pitched an idea based a unique product we had seen from a company only a few miles from our offices. It was called the Vision Dome.

Elumens was an RTP based startup that had attracted venture capital funding based on an optical lens patent and the design of the Vision Dome. The Vision Dome was like a mini IMAX theater comprised of an inflatable fabric shell that when erected would create a perfectly spherical screen surface. When used with a high resolution video projector fitted with a special fisheye lens, the screen created an immersive way to watch a video or interactive presentation. The product could fit into a reasonably small case and setup took only about 20 minutes.

We saw the Vision Dome as the ultimate tradeshow platform. Its presence alone was an eye turner, and we knew it would draw a crowd. We also knew that we could pull together a team to create a presentation that would take advantage of the unique format. With the client sold on the idea, we got to work on coming up with the storyline for the animation.

The Arris script would be a first person journey through a future house where the main character interacted with technology. This places the audience in a virtual home as if they were experiencing the interactive features of Arris first hand. The first person approach allowed us to avoid having to deal with rendering characters, which we knew we didn't have the time or resources to do. We knew we could have fun with the story as long as the simulations were believable, so we tried to make the idea of ordering a golf club, or checking a video voice mail as unique as possible. Some of the simulations were a little cheesy, but the point was very clear – the future would be a much more connected, interactive place. In addition to the first person segment of the script, the presentation would shift to a ride down the network to the network operations center where the servers and high speed broadband connections terminated. This brought to life the static network cloud diagrams traditionally used to explain the relationship and function of different components. In effect, we were attempting to take the audience on a ride with this piece, from the initial loading into the theater to the surrounding imagery and Dolby 5.1 soundtrack.

At VisionFactory part of our appeal was that we enjoyed taking on new challenges and working with emerging technologies. If we could find a new, different way to tell the client's story then we felt like we were doing our job. The client was happy to be breaking new ground just as we were. Also, we found that we could charge more for the learning curve in most cases. This made the Arris project the best of all worlds. It was extremely challenging and had a sizable budget.

Working with this new technology however wasn't a walk in the park. We found early on that the Elumins lens required a high resolution video source in order to present a decent image. Regular NTSC video at a resolution of 720x480 wasn't going to cut it. This was a time when HDTV was still emerging and wasn't the best option for what we were doing. Rather, playback from a dedicated PC was our best choice, but video codecs and processor speeds were still limited in their ability to play a high resolution clip smoothly. We were pushing our limits in lots of ways.

Elumins had a genius software guru and all around problem solver who provided a beta version of a video codec that helped us on the playback end. He also helped set us up with a plugin for LightWave3D and 3D Studio Max to render 3D environments that looked natural on the 180 degree VisionDome screen. The cobbled together software package was getting its first real world test with our ambitious project. The render intense project was made even more complicated by the huge frames that were required by the project and since this was around seven minutes or original animation, it required around 12,600 individual frames to be rendered on as many computers as we could link together on the network. Technically this was the most advanced project we had ever tried. It combined 3D animation, After Effects composites, live action video, and a Dolby 5.1 soundtrack. We dedicated about 10 people to the project over the course of a couple of months.

The Arris script was written in a Hollywood screenplay format in order to present the flow of the story and help the client to easily understand what they would be experiencing. It very easily could have been done in two columns, but the feel of the piece was like watching a movie and the screenplay format worked well both during the writing and during the actual production. The story is written to occupy an immersive projection environment, and when possible, the script attempted to exploit this environment. After all, it was the major selling point and point of attraction for the piece.

The Arris piece will always be one of my favorite projects because it presented so many insurmountable problems, yet we plowed though and delivered an amazing piece for the client. The entire VisionFactory team worked together like a well-tuned machine making the experience feel like what I think a 1930's Hollywood studio must have been like, with all departments pulling together until a movie was formed. The project was the result of our original vision for the company, a creative factory exploiting technology and imagination to tell stories.

Upon entering the VisionDome, users are completely drawn into its spherical structure, which forms a fully immersive 180 degree hemispheric screen. Users see vivid images which take on depth and reality via Elumens' unique optics. The VisionDome creates a reality-based environment that enhances the professional worker's quality and productivity.

Model VS3

All VisionDome systems are scalable and are designed to work with the most commonly used computing workstations: Intel® & Alpha®-based WindowsNT® PCs and Silicon Graphics® Workstations. Elumens' competitively priced systems provide for a complete, integrated solution that includes the VisionDome structure, patented optics, seamless screen, high-resolution projector, computer monitor, and software.

Contact Sales

Model V4

Model V5

Figure 7-1: This snap from the now defunct Elumens web page shows a few of the Visiondome designs. The Arris project utilized the V5, a 5 meter diameter dome that could accommodate many people during each showing.

Prologue: Entering the dome - THIS SECTION LOOPS UNTIL PRESENTATION IS STARTED   Steve's Script copy.

When groups of 7-8 enter the dome, they see three objects slowly rotating in 3D space on the center of the screen. These objects are blue wire-frame representations of:

    Voice- telephone handset
    Data - laptop
    Video - camcorder

Each of these objects occupies a distinct 1/3 of the screen, floating against the black space. Below the objects, receding into the deep space is an amber grid that **slowly** moves back providing the illusion of depth and movement.

There is a distinct audio ambience within the dome, comprised of both a musical undertone and sound sculpting.

Program begins - ARC OR VFI REPRESENATIVE ALWAYS STARTS PRESENTATION WHILE ACCOMPANIED BY ARRIS REPRESENATIVE.

The dome becomes completely dark and music pots up as the introduction begins. From just behind the lens, the 3wire-frame objects (telephone handset, laptop, camcorder) scream forward in the center of the dome one at a time cued as the Narrator speaks accompanied by sound fx.

                    NARRATOR VOICE ONE
          Three separate networks.

               Voice

The wire-frame telephone image becomes photo-realistic

                    NARRATOR VOICE ONE
               Video

The wire-frame camcorder image becomes photo-realistic

                    NARRATOR VOICE ONE

          And Data

The wire-frame laptop becomes photo-realistic. The three objects settle in the forward distance.

                    NARRATOR VOICE ONE
          Separate services,
          Separate networks
          But not for long!

The 3 images crash into each other creating a flash of white light
and crash of music. The ride pushes into a blinding tunnel of light
and data, as the "ride" through a broadband pipe begins. The pipe
takes quick turns as the audience is visually propelled into the
future of Broadband.

                    NARRATOR VOICE ONE
          The future of Broadband to the home.
          One Network.
          Converged services.
          Lighting speed, and
          Unlimited opportunity.

The ride settles on a mosaic of imagery, an endless sea of video,
data, photography, and end users interacting. The mosaic transforms
into the logos of Nortel Networks, Antec and Cornerstone
(subservient to Nortel Networks and Antec).

                    NARRATOR VOICE ONE
          End to end solutions today,
          And the vision for tomorrow.
          Nortel Networks and Antec.

          HFC solutions for the future.

End of Prologue

FADE IN:

1. Scene   Introduction – World is HVC Networked

The three company logos cross fade into a white screen opening to a view from space looking at the earth. A forward push takes us through the atmosphere, as the details of the continents become clear, then the details of North America.

The journey moves toward New Orleans as the image hits a cloudbank, clearing on the other side over a suburban neighborhood. The homes (many of them across the hilly terrain) are wire-frames at this point. Along the homes, following the connecting streets is the glowing trace of connectivity - the cable plant. These connecting lines illuminate with the network activity, as the camera glides above the neighborhood, just before diving toward the ground.

The camera "flies" close to the ground, following one street between the rows of homes. The cable connection points pass on either side of the frame. This flight continues momentarily until a final swoop takes us toward the outside of one house. There the flight rests on a box that is Converged Services Port branded as Cornerstone. (The glowing beams shooting in and out of the cable going into the box illustrate the network connectivity.)

> NARRATOR VOICE ONE
> Only one solution provides the home the
> true convergence of entertainment,
> telephony and Internet: HFC Networking

WHITE CROSS FADE to next screen

2. Scene Kitchen – Convergence of voice, video, data

White fades to reveal the inside of kitchen where audience sees a refrigerator, a window, and countertop with IP Phone. The room is clean and simple with no clutter.

The sound of whistling accompanies the protagonist POV entering the kitchen set. (Whistling and the character voice emanate from behind the audience to accent the illusion of first person POV.)

> RODERICK
> Activate House Agent

The POV moves closer to the IP phone unit (PROTOTYPE PROVIDED BY CLIENT) resting on the edge of the bar. The unit contains an integrated view-screen displaying an intuitive, simple GUI.

The camera dollies to the GUI with Bloomberg-like background on it. The Smart House interactive agent, GEA (an animated talking globe) swoops onto the screen. Protagonist POV continues SLOW movement in until phone GUI is in the center of the viewing screen. The view of the phone is slightly angled to the side, but viewer can still see the handset of it.

                           GEA
                 Voice Command Recognized.
                 Welcome home, RODERICK
                 Security system disarmed.

On the GUI, just beside of GEA, the "voice recognition icon" appears and a blueprint of the home displays red lines throughout the home turning to green lines. "Security Disabled" blinks three times then the blueprint collapses into a corner of the GUI.

                           GEA
                 Daily report: You have 35 new emails and
                 24 new video mails. I have eliminated
                 spam so you now have 1 video mail.

On the GUI: Thumbnail one with Caption "GLADICE WHILSHIRE -
(336) 555-7865"

                         RODERICK
                 Play Message.

The "voice recognition icon" blinks on screen showing command accepted by GEA.

The VideoMail menu opens onscreen to with viewing area of video with younger woman in front of lake holding a small child in her lap. The woman is pointing a remote to the camera before she begins speaking.

                          GLADICE
                 Hey honey. It's another beautiful
                 day here. Can't wait 'til you join
                 us this weekend. I'll send a video
                 of Kelly on the lake later- she has been swimming
                 like a fish!   Call us tonight.

                           KELLY
                 Bye Daddy!!!

The woman points the remote to the camera and videomail ends. The message box collapses. Remaining on the GUI is the evening's dinner menu complete with nutritional values and shopping list.

The camera POV leaves phone GUI, "looks up" and begins to travel toward the living room.

3. Scene: Living Room - Convergence of voice, video, data

The living room is very modern, sparsely decorated with unique furnishings, an easy chair, couch and a large display device on the main wall with environmental video.

There is a mechanical dog, Fido, sitting on a charging station in the corner of the room. When viewer enters room, Fido sits up on hind legs and begins begging.

FIDO

Bark. Bark. Whine. Bark.

RODERICK

Stay Fido

Fido "collapses" and sits back down in his charger - a rejected pet.

FIDO

Whine

Camera shows the POV of sitting on sofa facing the main screen, now dead center ahead (taking up a large portion of the VisionDome display area). The screen transforms from the painting to a dynamic user interface (main GUI).

GEA appears on the GUI accompanied by weather info, stock ticker, list of "links" to channels (news, sports, etc)

RODERICK

Start News Broadcast

The "voice recognition icon" blinks on screen showing command accepted by GEA.

4. Scene: Newscast - Ecommerce and Convergence

The GUI reforms to give the majority of space to a traditional television newscast with the News Anchor, a young African American

woman. Below this area, an integrated Banner Ad feature contextually
cycles throughout the broadcast.

                         NEWS ANCHOR
                  In business news, the continuing
                  revolution of network convergence

On GUI, "INCOMING VIDEOCALL" icon appears with name "RAY GLASS 919-
555-7777". All of this information is beside the ongoing newscast
which is unaffected by it's appearance.

                         made possible by HFC technology is
                         bringing new possibilities to the
                         broadband home.

Menu shows text box "Pause BROADCAST -- TAKE CALL?"

                         By integrating e-commerce, video on
                         demand, voice and video telephony
                         and many emerging data services, service providers
                         are breaking new ground in the way we communicate.

                         RODERICK

                  Pause Broadcast - Take Call"

The "voice recognition icon" blinks on screen showing command
accepted by GEA. Pause Icon appears over Newscast portion. News
section is "Paused" on still frame. New box appears under video
call menu with Ray sitting at desk and looking at screen.

                         RODERICK
                  Hello?

                              RAY
                  Hey Whilshire. I've got those file updates for
                  your approval. There's about 48 megs in all.

                         RODERICK
                  Great Ray. Can you send them on over?

                              RAY
                  Sure, one second.

Onscreen, beside Ray's video window an area forms with the header,
INCOMING FILES. Camera zooms into the area for incoming files until
it "goes through" the GUI. In 3D, 15 files/packets are seen
swooshing forward [NOTE: like going to light speed in Star Wars or
going to warp speed in Star Trek]. In the area a rapid-fire series

of time indicator bars pop up, zip through and close. All fifteen
bars come on and clear in a matter of seconds. Camera moves back
and the viewer is in front of screen again.

                         RODERICK
                    Got it.

                            RAY
                    Wow. That was fast. Let me know if
                    you need anything else.

                         RODERICK
                    Will do it. Thanks Ray.

                            RAY
                    Take Care and thanks

Ray moves forward to end call. Ray's window closes and PAUSE icon
over Newscast disappears. Newscast resumes from where paused
earlier.

                       NEWS ANCHOR
                    …The bottom line, big return on
                    investment and record breaking
                    growth. More in a moment.

The video screen dips to black and commercial for a golf club
begins. Video: Still shots on the golf course, with close-ups of
club, and the logo "SportSource" cut together.

                     COMMERCIAL VOICE
                    The SportSource Equalizer 99 is the world's
                    top performing laser enhanced club. Order yours
                    today from our website.

                         RODERICK
                    Go to Sportsource.com and find order form for
                    keyword, "Equalizer"

The "voice recognition icon" blinks on screen showing command
accepted by GEA. The ad shows still image of the Equalizer 99 and
PAUSE icon appears over box. A new second box opens with
SportSource order sheet on club.
                         RODERICK
                    Order one Equalizer and charge to house account

The "voice recognition icon" blinks on screen showing command
accepted by GEA.

                       SPORTSOURCE

Your order should arrive tomorrow. Thank you for
shopping SportSource.

> RODERICK
> Resume Broadcast.

The SportSource order window disappears. The pause icon over the
video window disappears and the image dips to black. The News
Broadcast resumes.

> NEWSANCHOR
> Now let's take a look at the nation's
> forecast, brought to you by Nortel
> Networks and Antec.

Below the newscast box, the banner ad reads "ONLINE UNIVERSITY:
LEARN MORE ABOUT HFC"

> RODERICK
> Go to OnLine University

The "voice recognition icon" blinks on screen showing command
accepted by GEA.

5. Scene: Distance Learning with Network Tour

The camera dollies toward the large screen while the screen fills
with the splash page for ONLINE University. The page animates on as
an announcer begins.

> ANNOUNCER
> Online University presents:
> "Learning more about HFC…featuring
> Billy, and The Professor!"

In time with the announcer the "Online UNIVERSITY" logo flies in,
followed by the lesson Title, then a cartoon-like still image of a
small boy, Billy, and a cartoon-like image of a Professor - nerdy,
with pocket protector, and wearing white coat.

> ANNOUNCER
> Should today's lesson be charged to house or
> business account?

> RODERICK

Charge to house account and begin lesson.

The "voice recognition icon" blinks on screen showing command accepted by GEA.

Character images fade away as the animation begins. The animation begins high in the sky to bring into view the relationship of the home, the cable service provider, an Application Service Provider and a Telephony Central Office. ***THIS IS THE SAME OPENING SEQUENCE AS SCENE ONE WITH OVERVIEW OF CITY. CAMERA DOES PUSH IN TO NEIGHBORHOOD DURING DIALOGUE.***

BILLY

Professor?   What does H-F-C mean?

PROFESSOR
HFC stands for Hybrid fiber/coax. It's a fancy name for combining the high bandwidth of fiber optic cable with the local CATV coax. This single network delivers telephone and high speed data service. Here's a look at how it works.

The camera moves steadily toward the wire-frame representation of broadband home ***(SAME IMAGE FROM THE SECURITY SEQUENCE FROM SCENE 2).*** There are wireless devices in three different rooms. The kitchen (an IP Phone), the living room (the large screen set), and the home office room (a laptop computer).

The connected objects stand out from the simple wire-framed house because they are fully shaded and colored, and each displays an example of video or data connectivity. The camera settles in front of the Converged Services Port on outside of house where these objects can be seen in the Background

The Converged Services Port becomes the center of attention and concentric semi-circles emanate from it indicating wireless transmission.

PROFESSOR
You see Billy, the Cornerstone Converged Services Port on the side of the house wirelessly connects to devices like your television, computer, and videophone.

BILLY
Really? How does it do it?

The Camera moves from the Converged Services Port, down along a FLEXIBLE coax run toward the Broadband Tap. The top half of the coax is translucent - allowing the data within to illuminate as we move along the path. It makes a turn as it follows the broadband tap toward the next element - the Digital Fiber Node.

                    PROFESSOR
          The coax at the Converged Services Port delivers
          high- speed data packets to the home by connecting
          to a digital fiber node in the local network.

The camera now passes by the fiber node to the Fiber cable, which feeds the optical data. This cable is different, there is much more data present; It allows massive throughput. The optical cable ride pulls away as we see the Cable Provider's Headend approaching - An industrial style building - The Service Provider.

                    PROFESSOR (cont.)
          This Device converts the high-bandwidth optical
          data packets, which arrive over fiber optic cable.
          At the headend, this fiber connects to the
          Cornerstone Super Access Node which routes the
          packets to the Secure Private Network System.

The Camera enters the wire-frame building and passes by the Optical Access Node toward the Secure Private Network System.

The Camera pulls back, overhead, to reveal the connectivity of An ISP to the right, a Network Cloud to the left and a Video Data center in the distance ahead. The Camera darts down toward the ISP, arriving close to the building to see inside a number of "floating" video images of web sites and end users.

                    PROFESSOR
          The fiber connection to an Internet Service
          Provider ensures high bandwidth access to all of
          the content and applications of the public
          Internet.

                    BILLY
          Wow, that's cool. But, what about telephone calls?

The camera returns to a point above the Secure Private Network System. It begins to dart to the left, following the data pipe to the Succession IP Telephony cloud.

                    PROFESSOR
          The Secure Private Network System also connects to
          the Succession IP Telephony Network which enables
          traditional voice calls, video telephony and other
          powerful applications.

Surrounding the network cloud is a number of video windows of end
users including a wireless caller, video conferencer and, laptop
user.

                        BILLY
            And what if I just want to watch TV?

The Camera returns to overhead and starts toward the building at the
center, the Video Data Center. As it gets closer the video windows
that appear all display entertainment programs, movies etc.

                        PROFESSOR
            The system also connects to a video center that
            enables live broadcasts and video on demand, stored
            on a cache server. This gives the viewer many ways
            to choose what they want to see, and when they want
            to see it.

The camera begins to pull away from the scene, slowly overhead.

                        BILLY
            Professor, who makes all of this possible?

The image slowly fades and is replaced by Nortel Networks and Antec
logos.

                        PROFESSOR
            The End to End solutions to make the broadband home
            a reality are made by Nortel Networks and Antec.

                        BILLY
            Golly! Thanks Professor.

                        PROFESSOR
            You're welcome Billy.

The online UNIVERSITY splash screen returns with text "15 edu-
credits now debited from house account".

                        ANNOUNCER
            Tomorrow's lesson on Online UNIVERSITY,
            "What ever happened to Satellite TV?"

Our Living room camera begins its pull out from the full screen and
back into the living room environment POV shot.

6. Scene: Order Movie
The Online splash screen dips to black and the main GUI screen
appears. Camera begins movement out and away from scene.

                          RODERICK
                     Go to Entertainment

GUI shows ENTERTAINMENT link enlarge to full screen with list of
selections: NEW: SPACE WAR CHAPTER 10, CLASSICS, WESTERNS, SCIFI,
YOUR FAVORITES, CARTOONS, OTHER

                          RODERICK
                 Download Space Wars Episode 10.

Fido barks and walks over to the couch. On the screen, the movie
begins. There is the distinct crawl of words on the screen (opening
of Star Wars.) Music here is faintly John Williams-like.

7. Scene: Conclusion - Neighborhood is networked

Move back from house interior, to see house exterior and box, then
neighborhood, then other neighborhoods, focusing on neighborhood
connectivity. (REVERSE OF SCENE ONE SEQUENCE)

                          NARRATOR
                 Broadband of the Future. Brought to
                 you by Nortel Networks and Antec.

                         FADE OUT

Chapter 10: The Strongest Link
Parody or Homage? The anatomy of a good pop culture rip-off

Bell and Howell is known to most people as the creator of the "Green Machine" 16mm Projectors from elementary school, at least for people of a certain age. To me, the company has a nostalgic link, not only for those clickity-clackity flicker machines, but for their little brothers – the wind up Bell and Howell Super-8 camera and black silent projector I grew up with. I can thank the company for my first ever experiences watching and making a real film.

Jumping ahead to modern times, Bell and Howell has become a much different company. Known now as Bowe Bell and Howell, the company transitioned it's mechanical creations into massive publishing machinery that allow large companies to print on demand things like brochures, mailers, bills, and even books. The highly complex devices can easily fill a large room, and their operation is a site to behold. At one end a huge roll of paper feeds the beast of rollers, printers, folders, glue applicators, heaters, presses and cutters, and out the other end comes customized individual publications. In many ways it is logical to see how this evolved from something like a film projector. It's also easy to see how this type of machine means big business to the company.

Fortunately for me, Bowe Bell and Howell had a manufacturing facility only a few miles from the VisionFactory offices and their marketing director had become interested in our work. As the marketing director for a large company, she had an enormous amount of projects to coordinate. Part of these included creating compelling tradeshow content to attract potential customers to buy the BBH document machines. Understandably, it was difficult to transport and setup these machines the several tradeshows each year. Logistics and expense limited their tradeshow presence.

Our challenge was to help the client create an entertaining way to explain the benefits of these machines and the value of working with BBH as a partner. We wanted to have a presentation that included a live presentation via an onsite host, and elements of a video that the host could interact with. These types of presentations would often run on a set schedule at a tradeshow – every 15 minutes or so. We worked with the client on several ideas and finally agreed on a unique take of a popular game show called "The Weakest Link". The live presenter would gather an audience in a seating area, begin the presentation and then hand off to a canned video game show at different intervals. There would also be an element of audience participation and prizes would be given to the participants. The goal would be to entice an audience to spend time at the BBH booth, hopefully entertain them while they were there, and of course, drill home the positive message about how good the products and the company were.

"The Weakest Link" was a hit NBC primetime game show that originated in Great Britain. The abrasive British host would routinely insult the contestants in the trivia based contest as the weakest ones were eliminated. Ultimately the last contestant standing would be the winner. The show had a winning formula and was ripe for parody. The client was fully onboard with creating a video that stole as much as possible from this format. The trivia based element of the game allowed us to plug in already established marketing points about the company and its products, and we knew we could keep the pace going quickly, hoping not to lose our captive audience's attention.

The idea of parody or homage seems to be the first thing that a client comes up with when brainstorming a project like this. Before this project we had completed a Star Wars parody for a live presentation, a Mission Impossible themed animation for a Nortel Product, video game parody for an interactive training piece, an elaborate Jurassic Park parody shot on location in Jasper Park Lodge in Canada, and many others subtle rip-offs. It seems that the shorthand of starting from a common reference point always helped the ideas flow and the agreement happen faster. Also, for the scripting process, an idea like a game show parody provided the essential structure. In the case of our new project which had now become "The Strongest Link", the scripting process was a straight forward act of filling in the blanks and trying to be a little tongue in cheek with our host and three contestants.

The production design was another challenge that we had to solve. We knew we needed a studio to make this a convincing production. We needed a set, good lighting and we had to cast our three contestants and host. Having both the TV series as a reference and artwork from the client, we set out to create a production design that used as many elements as possible to create high production value and consistent messaging. Our biggest coup was finding a local production studio with a dormant set from an old PBS game show. The main elements were there – podiums, background elements, even some funky tech-like set pieces. This was the key to making our vision look like we wanted. Although we were operating on a limited budget, we secured the location and decided to use the three studio cameras and live switcher to shoot the bulk of the action. We also used a small Canon DV camera on a jib for a few shots. Amazingly, the Canon mounted on a jib held its own against the seventy- thousand dollar studio cams.

The in house producer for VisionFactory was an extremely talented woman who managed the preproduction of this project in a way that the actual shoot was a joy. All of the artwork, set dressing, costumes and other logistics had to come together and synch so that the actual on camera time was spent creating what was on the script, and not chasing down little problems. Fortunately, the producer also created some great support documents along the way and I am including them here along with the script which I created. I'm also providing some of the artwork that we used for the shoot and in the development of the tradeshow booth.

Before diving into the development documents, I want to explore once again the idea of layers or production. This project juggled many realities at once, each requiring precise communication, timing, technology, and performance. All of these are coordinated with scripts which had to be created. The complexity of a project like is an ambitious challenge, but when done well can really give the client something unique. So by coordinating all of these layers – the live presentations, the interactive video clips, the actual production of the game show, and the audience interactions – we helped the client achieve their goal of engaging high value customers in an entertaining way, hopefully leading to ultimate sales of their very expensive products. After all of the fun, it comes down to ROI – return on investment for the client, and with "The Strongest Link", that was our ultimate goal. The fun along the way was just a bonus.

Logo Design

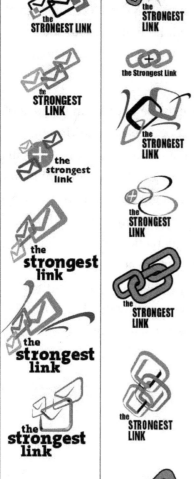

Our graphic designer came up with many logo options based on the Bowe Bell & Howell themes and the art of The Weakest Link game show.

The final logo below was the ultimate winner. This design was integrated into the video segments, questions used within the game show, set design and actual tradeshow booth. The quality of the graphics illustrates how different talents within the production team can combine to make a polished final piece.

Once the logo design was chosen, it was incorporated into the set via some custom print work onto foam core. The results looked very professional and instantly made the set our own.

Following is a copy of the original proposal document prepared for the client. It was very thorough in both laying out the requirements and scope of the project as well as detailing the budget.

Bell+Howell

Mail and Messaging Technologies

Xplor 2001 Video Presentation

Work Description and Proposal

Submitted by VisionFactory, Inc.

visionfactory

Overview

This document is VisionFactory, Inc.'s (hereafter VFI) response to Bell+Howell's (hereafter BH) request for a proposal for the creation of a video-based presentation that for use in the Xplor2001 and NPF 2002 Tradeshow events.

This document has been developed by VFI to provide an outline of the core requirements, as VFI understands them and an accompanying budget consistent with the project's creative design and implementation.

Target Audiences	• Potential new customers attending tradeshow event • Existing BH customers attending tradeshow event
Functional Objectives	• Media presentation will be displayed on large Tobisha monitor (specs to be provided by BH's equipment manager) and two plasma screens. • Deliverables include: (2) CD-ROMs with final media presentation files and the final files loaded on the BH provided Dell workstations (purchased by BH for playback of VFI produced media for the Xplor 2000 and NPF 2001 events)
Design Requirements	• The maximum length of entire presentation is 10 minutes • The live presenter (C.C.) must be incorporated into the presentation • The presentation should be "motivational, fast-paced, and exciting" • The media will use BH approved colors and branding • The presentation will be video based with graphic and animation support • The presentation will be a parody of the current NBC game show, "Weakest Link' with British host Anne Robison. (Images of the show's set, graphics, and host included at the end of this document.) • The BH video will have "The Strongest Link" game show with 2 (maximum of 3 contestants) and a female host (total of maximum 4 on screen talent) • The full script will be written using the script treatment document provided by BH to Megan Bell on August 2, 2001. • *There will be a maximum of four questions for the contestants. With each question, the same character will provide the correct answer (which involves using BH and Jet product services).* • *There will be brief animation sequences showing the products*

from the "correct" answer. The "product" animation sequences will play on the two outer plasma screens while the main video will play on the center screen.

• The self-contained video will incorporate pre-recorded narration with C.C., the BH selected live presenter at the show.

• The media is not product focused, but line of business and services focused.

Deliverables

This proposal encompasses the following labor types and media deliverables.

Project Management and Video Producer

Concept development, Script writing, storyboard sketches

Video Director, BetaSP tape stock, and supporting graphics for one day shoot at closed studio with "game show" set

Set decorations and contestant podiums

Video Director/Cameraman, Grip, and video equipment (camera, lights, BetaSP tape stock, cabling) for half day shoot at BH offices to record b-roll of BH and Jet products

Video post production editing to create final media

Scoring (music and sound effects) for all media elements

Creation of original graphic elements (game show elements and product animation components)

Creation of original animation using graphic elements (game show elements and product animation sequences)

Integration and programming to combine all media elements (visual and audible)

Creation of CD-ROM with final file

Installation of final file on BH provided Dell workstations

On site support (one person for 4 days including 1 ½ days of travel and 2 ½ days on site), Oct 26 –29, 2001

Schedule

To ensure meeting BH's delivery due date and schedule, timely client responsiveness is critical. Should due dates or timelines be missed, the delivery date will be negatively impacted and additional costs will be incurred and billed to Bell+Howell. Final delivery of a CD-ROM with all media files will be October 15, 2001.

August 6 - 10	• Signed contract and PO issued • Job number assigned, job begins • Kick off meeting with Bell+Howell and VFI primes
Aug 13 - 17	• Concept development • Script writing, set and storyboard sketches • Studio inspection, studio reserved • Video equipment and crew reserved • Video set and set pieces reserved • Actors reserved for game show shoot
Aug 20 - 24	• Background templates and design comps for presentation provided • Music composition begins • Graphic design and animation work for presentation • Video shoot at BH offices (b-roll) • Final script approved by client • Sound studio recording session with CC reserved
Aug 27 - 31	• Testing of Final Presentation programming • Final Delivery to client of CDROM with all media presentation files
Sept 3	• LABOR DAY HOLIDAY
Sept 6	• Pre-production of game show set
Sept 7	• Game Show Video Shoot
Sept 10 - 28	• Sound recording session with CC (and post work) • Video edit • Animation complete and integrated • Score complete and integrated • Graphics complete and integrated • Client review and revisions sessions of all media
Oct 12	• Client signoff of final media
Oct 15 - 16	• Final media presented to client on CD-ROM • Final media presentation installed on BH provided Dell workstations
Oct 17	• (3) Workstations shipped to event with BH shipping account information
Oct 26 - 28	• On site support personnel at Xplor event

Budget & Invoicing

The budget for developing the presentation media elements described in this document (with development timeframe from August 2001 to October 2001) is $65,000.

The projected budget does not include:

- *Shipping, freight, tonnage, or any other equipment moving related expense, which if incurred, will result in client approval prior to purchase and separate invoice(s)*
- *Any travel costs for on site support personnel (transportation, lodging, food) which will be invoiced to the client after completion of trip*

This project will have two types of billings.

- *First, services directly provided by VFI will be billed as one fee to BH. **The total amount due to VFI for the services described herein is $51,000.***
- *Secondly, services selected by VFI for the project will be billed individually to BH as incurred. **The total amount for vendor services billed directly to BH is $14,000.***

The invoices for the $52,000 to VFI will be issued as follows with Net 20 terms:
- *Retainer fee of $12,000 issued with signed approval of this document (August 10, 2001)*
- *Second installment of $10,000 issued August 31, 2001*
- *Third installment of $10,000 issued September 17, 2001*
- *Fourth installment of $10,000 issued October 8, 2001*
- *Final installment of $ 9,000 issued November 5, 2001*

For the vendor services selected by VFI for the project that will directly bill BH, each individual vendor will issue invoicing to BH. The companies expected at this time to bill BH directly include: Take One Productions (studio and equipment rental for game show shoot), Soundtrax (sound recording studio rental for CC recording), StageWorks (for special lighting for game show set), and Capital Artists (for on-screen talent). Should the total billings from outside vendors exceed the VFI provided estimate of $14,000, VFI will deduct the difference from the final VFI invoice (November 5, 2001).

Acceptance

Please sign and submit to indicate your acceptance of this proposal and the terms therein.

_____

Concept Images

These images are from the NBC Weakest Link website.

VFI Process

VFI recognizes that providing a strategic solution requires a strong process methodology and commitment to extending that approach to every initiative. This iterative, evolving process fosters interactive collaboration to enhance our partnership and produce outstanding results.

Stage 1: Discover

VFI will meet with your team to assess the project's unique requirements. During this phase, VFI will collaborate with Bell+Howell to list specific project objectives and to agree on the solution design. From these project objectives, VFI will produce a high level project plan and a scope of work for Bell+Howell to review and approve.

Stage 2: Design

With the vision and needs of the Bell+Howell clearly defined, specific project teams are designated. The final "blueprint" for all components of the VFI suggested solution, including design and programming for the project (features and functionality, plans, budget, etc.) are provided.

Stage 3: Develop

During this phase, VFI will produce and manage the development of all components of the project. All development milestones include regularly scheduled formal internal and external reviews to ensure that all project deliverables meet the highest standards of quality and meet or exceed expectations.

Stage 4: Deploy

At this stage, VFI will conduct integration testing to ensure that all elements work seamlessly as a turnkey solution. VFI will also address any technical issues uncovered during testing and reintegrate the media in iterative cycles until all issues are successfully resolved.

Stage 5: Deliver

During the final development stage, VFI will provide required training and coordinate applicable co-marketing activities.

Studio Quote and Concept image

The next document is a quote for studio space at a local production facility that was once a local TV station. As mentioned before, we found way more than our money's worth from this location since there was a complete game show set from a previous production available.

This quote is followed by a series of power point slides that were prepared for the client to help visualize the production. This was also used in helping the set designer and graphic designer to prepare the materials needed to create the look we were after in the studio.

PRODUCTIONS

8/16/01

Vision Factory

3 camera studio shoot revised quote

Studio rental set up day	250.00
Paint touch up	200.00
Assistant producer for set up	250.00
Studio rental shoot day	550.00
3 camera shoot / 3 operators	2400.00
Audio w / 4 lavaliers	600.00
Gaffer	400.00
Make up	500.00

Sub total	$ 5,150.00

Tape beta sp 30 @ 42.00 each

These prices are based on a 10 hr day.

Studio is not sound proof. Interruptions may occur.

½ payment due upon booking of facility.

½ payment due upon completion of shoot.

Also, do you need us to handle snacks and lunch?

Graphic Design Style and Potential Set Pieces

1. Weakest Link Logo and Host

2. Weakest Link Set

3. Potential Set Pieces (contestant stands)

*vision*factory

160

Elliptical Counter

The Script

Since this production was a sort of hybrid presentation, the script was created in a couple of different ways. The dialogue for the game show was written in a screenplay layout and the final overall script was done in a two column format. As with most of the writing I did at VisionFactory, the format wasn't chosen based on some industry standard, but rather what seemed to work for the team involved. Following are two versions of the script for "The Strongest Link". In the supplemental material you will find the finished segments of the game show that were created in during the studio shoot.

SUMMARY:

There are 3 screens at the tradeshow booth. The media in this script is for the CENTER screen. A screensaver will be made for the outer screens using the same flash animations from the center.

There will be 2 versions of the scripted media.

1. Live presenter (CC) with technical director hitting the space bar on certain cue points at the show event and ending with audience participation (AS SCRIPTED)

2. Standalone with piece running from start to finish by itself (ending with game show)

Two types of scenes – VIDEO and FLASH.

	SCENE DESCRIPTION	FLASH	VIDEO
1	CC Show intro	X	
2	Game Show Open		X
3	Question 1		X
4	Question 1 Wrap Up	X	
5	Question 2		X
6	Question 2 Wrap Up	X	
7	Question 3		X
8	Question 3 Wrap Up	X	
9	Throw Off Sam		X
9a	Sam's Confession		X
10	Question 4		X
11	Question 4 Wrap Up	X	
12	George Wins		X
13	Audience Participation		X
14	CC Audience Quiz	X	.
15	CC Wrap Up	X	

EACH SCENE WILL START AND END WITH STRONGEST LINK LOGO and music cue.

Tone & Pacing – fast, energetic, fun

This media is to entertain – not go into product details.

NOTES: graphics in green, programming in red

AUDIO	FLASH/PROGRAMMING	VIDEO
LOOP	**LOOP**	
Screensaver	Flash animation loop of **Strongest Link logo** and **BH logo**	
Scene 1: **FLASH INTRO SECTION**	**Flash**	
Dramatic MUSIC bumpers builds to a climax.	**Spacebar cue** Fade in.	
	A series of **background graphic elements** slide into place as music builds equally slowly. These can be shapes of different sized and colors...envelope shapes/pieces of the logo	
MUSIC highlights the animation.		
FANFARE accompanies the game show logo and music holds on a steady dramatic rumble.	The image becomes clear – it is the **Bell & Howell logo**. The Word **"PRESENTS"** slides into the composition.	
	With a musical kick – almost a fanfare – the screen is overtaken by the logo **"THE STRONGEST LINK"**.	
	The Flash piece continues as C.C. introduces herself and welcomes the crowd.	
CC: Ladies and gentlemen welcome to Xplor 2001 and the Bell & Howell experience. We're here to show you how Bell & Howell solutions are the strongest link between you and your customers. The strongest link to quality and profitability and the strongest	The Flash element remains on "THE STRONGEST LINK" title. There are animated elements that keep it interesting. **SPACEBAR CUE** Also there are the subtle	

AUDIO	FLASH/PROGRAMMING	VIDEO
link to a successful future. We all face many challenges. Challenges like postal rate hikes, rising costs and tight budgets, new government regulations, and the need for increased personalization of our mailings…all of this, with ever increasing mail and transaction volumes. Production managers need timely, accurate data to successfully meet their cost, quality, and customer service goals. Let's face it, with more complex operations and higher customer expectations, existing manual methods of production data collection are no longer sufficient. To help our customers meet these production challenges, Bell & Howell now offers a new generation of comprehensive production management systems and customer integration services. The systems provide a flexible "umbrella" of automation that integrates data across any production workflow and any type of equipment or process. Bell and Howell solutions and services also make it easy to respond to growing customer demand for electronic delivery of documents for the internet. Now let's join the game to learn more about these exciting solutions.	presence of keywords cycling. These are: Quality, Efficiency, Personalization, Real time data, Real time tracking *Spacebar cue* The Flash background remains the same, but the foreground assembles the CHALLENGES slide which includes images of dollar signs appearing over a messaging operation graphic, stacks of paper work, lots of envelopes, computers, lots of people – showing demands of today. *Spacebar cue* Stills from production manager software (scan from client brochures) *Spacebar cue* Bell & Howell logo animates onto the upper left of the screen. Then a series of scrolling text and accompanying images layer on. Green Digital Text (ticker bar) scroll includes: e-Jets JETSentry JETPlan TransFormer eMessaging JETrak IntellaSert	

AUDIO	FLASH/PROGRAMMING	VIDEO
	IntellaScan AV JETCost Enterprise Integration Solutions **Spacebar cue** Strongest Link show logo	
Scene 2: **THE GAMESHOW**		**THE STRONGEST** **LINK Set**
SHOW NARRATOR: And now, from our studios in beautiful downtown Burbankit's **The Strongest Link**!		Strongest Link show logo animation – then video of set floor.... (jib shot with floor director/smoke/studio cameras, etc)
HOST (GRETCHEN GRAVELY): Greeting audience and welcome to The Strongest Link. I am your host Gretchen Gravely, and today we are joined by three production managers, each hoping that he is the Strongest link. They are, Manny Middle.		Host Close UP Angle on MANNY
MANNY: Hello Gretchen.		Host Close up
HOST: George Jetson.		Angle on GEORGE
GEORGE: Good to be here.		Host close up
HOST: ...and, Sam Silo.		Angle on SAM
SAM: Sam I am, Gretchen.		

AUDIO	FLASH/PROGRAMMING	VIDEO
HOST: Now audience, pay attention, because your chance to play is coming up. Let's see who is The Strongest Link. MUSIC cues the setup for first question	Spacebar cue	Back on GRETCHEN. THE STRONGEST LINK logo overtakes screen.
Scene 3: QUESTION 1		**THE STRONGEST LINK Set**
HOST: Question one. In a very competitive environment, strong customer relationships are key to success. What are you doing to make your customer service a competitive advantage? Sam! SAM: Well, um, we…we've got really friendly folks on the phone - we try to handle every complaint that- HOST: Time's up! Manny! MANNY: We're looking for ways to cut our late deliveries, and we're thinking about adding online messaging. HOST: How, nice. George! GEORGE: We track the status of every job, from arrival to shipping. And we're so confident of our ability to deliver on-time, we		Set establishing shot Close up of HOST Cut to SAM in medium shot Sam is startled by the rudeness. Back on HOST Cut to MANNY Back on HOST Cut to GEORGE

AUDIO	FLASH/PROGRAMMING	VIDEO
offer our customers the opportunity to view the status of their job via the internet. HOST: Do you indeed? George, you are The Strongest link!	 Spacebar cue	HOST
Scene 4: **Q1 WRAP UP**	**Flash**	
C.C.: George was the Strongest Link this round. His clients can securely monitor their job progress via the Internet through secure links to live production data. George can track the status of jobs through all steps in the production process; he can also assess the impact of production delays and take corrective actions in time to keep his deliveries on schedule. Finally, George can provide personalized messages to his customers via both paper and the Internet.	The Strongest link logo in fullscreen. It transitions to Bell & Howell. Spacebar cue Then shows text of • Internet inquiry • On-time delivery • Paper or electronic format Spacebar cue Green Digital Text (ticker bar) scroll includes: e-Jets JETsentry JETplan TransFormer eMessaging Spacebar cue	Video/graphics showing… Customer viewing status of job via Internet…customer service rep pulling up data of job status in real time
Scene 5: **QUESTION 2**		**THE STRONGEST LINK Set**
HOST: Now George, you were the	Strongest Link Logo	Set establishing shot HOST CU

AUDIO	FLASH/PROGRAMMING	VIDEO
strongest link, Manny, you fell miserably behind and Sam – a pathetic last place.		Angle on SAM Angle on MANNY HOST close up
MUSIC bumper readies us for the next question.		
HOST: Contestants, Growing volume and the demand for personalization have made it more difficult to maintain integrity and operate efficiently. How can you ensure quality of output while improving your operations? Sam!		Show entire set with all contestants and host
SAM: Well, we work around the clock to make up for our mistakes.		SAM
HOST: Manny!		HOST
MANNY: (looks proud) We've hired a small army of people to perform manual quality checks regularly. When they all show up, we really don't miss that many…of course, it does slow down our processing a little.		MANNY
HOST: George!		HOST
GEORGE: First of all, our systems are faster and more efficient than ever, allowing us to do more with fewer resources. In addition, we've automated mail piece tracking and		GEORGE

AUDIO	FLASH/PROGRAMMING	VIDEO
integrity, eliminating manual quality checks – These steps have made it possible to increase production and quality at the same time, without increasing production costs. HOST: George, you are correct. Manny and Sam, you *might* qualify for the toddler version of our game.	 **Spacebar cue**	HOST Set establishing shot Strongest Link logo
Scene 6: **Q2 WRAP UP**	Flash	
C.C.: Once again, George is the strongest link. By incorporating highly efficient inserting systems he has managed to maintain costs and process higher volumes. In addition, automatically tracking and reconciling each mail piece eliminates the need for manual checks. Now operators spend less time manually tracking envelopes or locating that missing mailpiece. Each mailpiece can be tracked through the process to ensure accuracy of delivery and of content, including personalized inserts. This ensures that each customer receives all of their mail, and only their mail.	The **Strongest link logo** in fullscreen. It transitions to **Bell & Howell**. **Spacebar cue** **Tracking** **Integrity** **Spacebar cue** Green Digital Text (ticker bar) scroll includes: **JETrak** **IntellaSert** **IntellaScan AV** **Spacebar cue**	
Scene 7:		**THE STRONGEST**

AUDIO	FLASH/PROGRAMMING	VIDEO
QUESTION 3		**LINK Set**
HOST: Contestants, speaking of eliminating quality problems, it is now time for our elimination round. That is when we do everyone a favor and send one of you home. The question is, how can you be sure you are running your operations as cost efficiently and profitably as possible? Sam!		Stongest Link logo Establishing set shot Host Close up
SAM: Pass.		SAM looks blankly, puts his hand to his head. Thinks a moment. Pauses.
HOST: Manny!		HOST
MANNY: We use the clear and accurate data from the forms that our operators fill out, then we take the square footage of our operation center times pi and divide that by our CEO's daily caloric intake to determine the derivative of the….(cut off by Host)		MANNY
HOST: (interrupts) Manny you frighten me. George!		HOST
GEORGE: We stay profitable through real-time tracking, efficient job scheduling and accurate, up to the minute job costing. This is all automated for us		GEORGE

AUDIO	FLASH/PROGRAMMING	VIDEO
and available at the touch of a button. HOST: You are correct. I wish I could say the same for your competitors.	Spacebar cue	HOST Strongest Link logo
Scene 8: **Q3 WRAP UP**	**Flash**	
CC: (soft narration) Once again, George was the strongest link. He uses production management software to efficiently plan, schedule and execute new orders; and since his scheduling software is integrated with the real-time job tracking system, he can react quickly to changes on the production floor. And with job costing software that also integrates with his production data, he can accurately determine the costs of each job based on actual resources used.	The Strongest link logo in fullscreen. It transitions to Bell & Howell. Spacebar cue Job scheduling Job costing Spacebar cue Green Digital Text (ticker bar) scroll includes: JETplan JETcost	Video/graphics showing….show customer calling in with new job, service rep plugging it in to schedule & results…or production manager on job cost screen
Scene 9: **THROW OFF SAM**		**THE STRONGEST LINK Set**
HOST: The moment of truth has arrived. Sam, to put it kindly, you were not the Strongest	Spacebar cue	Strongest Link logo HOST then SAM

AUDIO	FLASH/PROGRAMMING	VIDEO
Link. In fact you've set a new low for performance on this show. I am pleased you are good at something. Goodbye!!		Sam has a dejected look as he is rejected. He walks by the others, head hanging in shame.
Scene 9a: **SAM'S CONFESSION**		**THE STRONGEST LINK Set**
SAM: You know, I guess I'm not a very good production manager. I need a new career. Maybe I'll become a game show host.		Close up of Sam with set and remaining contestants Strongest Link logo
Scene 10: **QUESTION 4**		**THE STRONGEST LINK Set**
HOST: George and Manny. A duo yes, but not so dynamic. This is our final question. Contestants, As a production manager, how do you manage the integration of all the technologies required to meet the challenges of a high-volume automated document factory? Manny! MANNY: Well, I'm personally responsible for all of our technology integration. I find it very simple- all technology is basically the same. Once you find the gizmo that connects the whatsit valve, you pretty much have it licked…unless of course, it has a…(cut off by host)	Spacebar cue	Establishing shot of set HOST Angle on MANNY

AUDIO	FLASH/PROGRAMMING	VIDEO
HOST: (looks disgusted with Manny, then turns) George! GEORGE: I know my strengths are in managing a highly complex production environment; I don't have time to worry about multiple vendor technology integration. I have selected a vendor that takes care of all of that for me. They consult with me to determine what our operations require, make recommendations, and manage the implementation of integrated solutions customized to our needs. HOST: George, you are correct.	 **Spacebar cue**	HOST Angle on GEORGE HOST **Strongest Link logo**
Scene 11: **Q4 WRAP UP**	**Flash**	
C.C. George is once again the strongest link. He has a partner that provides consultation, makes recommendations, and implements custom integrated solutions to provide an Automated Document Factory based on his requirements. His production management software links all of the elements of his operation including devices from a variety of vendors. And a	The **Strongest link logo** in fullscreen. It transitions to **Bell & Howell**. **Spacebar cue** **Integrated Solutions** **Flexibility with** **customized peripherals** **Across multiple devices** **Across multiple vendors** **Upgradability** **Spacebar cue** Green Digital Text (ticker bar) scroll includes: **JETS**	

AUDIO	FLASH/PROGRAMMING	VIDEO
modular approach to software implementation enables scalability and upgradability.	JETS & Inserters & Sorters Automated print-on-demand book w/AVS & Jets Spacebar cue	
Scene 12: **GEORGE WINS**		**THE STRONGEST LINK Set**
HOST: Once again, George was the strongest link. Manny, thank you for playing our game, but the customers have spoken. Goodbye. George, your grasp of an efficient, flexible and profitable automated document factory has proven you are the strongest link. GEORGE: Thanks Gretchen.	GEORGE, he smiles, leans in Spacebar cue	Strongest Link logo Estab shot of set HOST On MANNY HOST GEORGE HOST GEORGE
Scene 13: **AUDIENCE PARTICIPATION**		**THE STRONGEST LINK Set**

AUDIO	FLASH/PROGRAMMING	VIDEO
HOST: Now audience, it's you turn to play. You have been provided with a paper and pencil. Let me state this now. No chewing of the pencils. You will be asked four questions, at the end of which we will see who truly is the strongest link. Are you ready?		HOST, addressing the camera Logo overtakes the screen NOTE: Standalone version ends here with video of set then BH logo LIVE version continues as scripted.
	Spacebar cue	
Scene 14 C.C.'S AUDIENCE QUIZ	Flash	

AUDIO	FLASH/PROGRAMMING	VIDEO
A TICKING MUSIC cue begins C.C.: 1. Audience, what Bell & Howell suite of production management software links to any type of machine, old or new, from any manufacturer? BOATS? TRUCKS? JETS?	Spacebar cue The Strongest Link logo Spacebar cue QUESTION ONE: What Bell & Howell suite of production management software links to any type of machine, old or new, from any manufacturer? Spacebar cue *(question starts as full screen then shrinks to make room for answers)* Answers: • Boats Spacebar cue • Trucks Spacebar cue • Jets AIRFORCE JETS fly across the screen with jet sounds	
Question two. What intelligent inserter effectively handles multiple-set-size, high-page-count documents at consistently high throughput speeds.	Spacebar cue Question TWO. What intelligent inserter effectively handles multiple-set-size, high-page-count documents at consistently high throughput speeds. *(question starts as full screen then shrinks to make room for answers)* Answers: • BH 3Ke	

AUDIO	FLASH/PROGRAMMING	VIDEO
BH 3Ke BH 4Ke BH 12Ke	Spacebar cue • BH 4Ke Spacebar cue • BH 12Ke Spacebar cue carton of a dozen eggs Spacebar cue	
Question three. What "T" links the paper-based and electronic messaging worlds by creating and designing output in the formats you choose? Answers: Converter Renovator TransFormer	Question three. What "T" links the paper-based and electronic messaging worlds by creating and designing output in the formats you choose? *(question starts as full screen then shrinks to make room for answers)* Answers: • Converter Spacebar cue • Renovator Spacebar cue • TransFormer Spacebar cue show electronic transformer., or toy transformer?? Spacebar cue	
Question four: What Bell & Howell group provides consultive services, multiple-vendor contracting and customized solution for special applications?	Question four: What Bell & Howell group provides consultive services, multiple-vendor contracting and customized solution for special applications? *(question starts as full screen then shrinks to*	

AUDIO	FLASH/PROGRAMMING	VIDEO
	make room for answers)	
	Spacebar cue Answers: <ul><li>IRS (Integration Really Siloed)</li></ul> **Spacebar cue** <ul><li>FBI (Fully Botched Integration)</li></ul> **Spacebar cue** <ul><li>EIS (Enterprise Integration Solutions)</li></ul> **Spacebar cue**	
SCENE 15: Conclusion	**Flash**	
CC: George was the strongest link in our show today because he had all of the processes in place to meet his goals of reduced costs, higher quality, and top-notch customer service across an ADF environment. But you can all be winners because Bell & Howell has the products to support all of these processes. If you'd like to see how George accomplished his goals, follow our "links' to the area of your choice and our representatives will help you. *MARY Y – ANYTHING ABOUT HOW TO TURN IN ANSWER CARDS TO FOUND OUT WHO WINS??*	**Strongest Show Logo** **reduced costs, higher quality, and top-notch customer service across an ADF environment** **Bell & Howell** **Strongest Show Logo**	

SCENE ONE:

Ladies and gentlemen welcome to Xplor 2001 and the Bell & Howell experience. We're here to show you how Bell & Howell solutions are the strongest link between you and your customers. The strongest link to quality and profitability and the strongest link to a successful future. We all face many challenges. Challenges like postal rate hikes, rising costs and tight budgets, new government regulations, and the need for increased personalization of our mailings…all of this, with ever increasing mail and transaction volumes.

Production managers need timely, accurate data to successfully meet their cost, quality, and customer service goals. Let's face it, with more complex operations and higher customer expectations, existing manual methods of production data collection are no longer sufficient.

To help our customers meet these production challenges, Bell & Howell now offers a new generation of comprehensive production management systems and customer integration services. The systems provide a flexible "umbrella" of automation that integrates data across any production workflow and any type of equipment or process. Bell and Howell solutions and services also make it easy to respond to growing customer demand for electronic delivery of documents for the internet.

Now let's join the game to learn more about these exciting solutions.

SCENE TWO:

George was the Strongest Link this round. His clients can securely monitor their job progress via the Internet through secure links to live production data.

George can track the status of jobs through all steps in the production process; he can also assess the impact of production delays and take corrective actions in time to keep his deliveries on schedule.

Finally, George can provide personalized messages to his customers via both paper and the Internet.

SCENE SIX:

Once again, George is the strongest link. By incorporating
highly efficient inserting systems he has managed to maintain
costs and process higher volumes. In addition, automatically
tracking and reconciling each mail piece eliminates the need
for manual checks. Now operators spend less time manually
tracking envelopes or locating that missing mailpiece.

Each mailpiece can be tracked through the process to ensure
accuracy of delivery and of content, including personalized
inserts. This ensures that each customer receives all of
their mail, and only their mail.

SCENE EIGHT:

(soft narration) Once again, George was the strongest link.
He uses production management software to efficiently plan,
schedule and execute new orders; and since his scheduling
software is integrated with the real-time job tracking system,
he can react quickly to changes on the production floor. And
with job costing software that also integrates with his
production data, he can accurately determine the costs of each
job based on actual resources used.

SCENE NINE:

George is once again the strongest link. He has a partner
that provides consultation, makes recommendations, and
implements custom integrated solutions to provide an Automated
Document Factory based on his requirements.

His production management software links all of the elements
of his operation including devices from a variety of vendors.
And a modular approach to software implementation enables
scalability and upgradability.

Cast Script for Studio Shoot
Scene 2: THE GAMESHOW

SHOW NARRATOR:
And now, from our studios in beautiful downtown Orlando, it's
The Strongest Link!

HOST (GRETCHEN GRAVELY):
Greeting audience and welcome to The Strongest Link. I am
your host Gretchen Gravely, and today we are joined by three
production managers, each hoping that he is the Strongest
link. They are, Manny Middle.

MANNY:

Hello Gretchen.

HOST:

George Jetson.

GEORGE:

No relation.

HOST:

…and, Sam Silo.   Now audience, pay attention, because your
chance to play is coming up.

Let's see who is The Strongest Link!!

Scene 3: QUESTION 1

HOST:

Question one.   In a very competitive environment, strong
customer relationships are key to success.   What are you doing
to make your customer service a competitive advantage?   Sam!

SAM:

Well, um, we…we've got really friendly folks on the phone - we
try to handle every complaint that-

HOST:

Time's up! Manny!

MANNY:

We're looking for ways to cut our late deliveries, and we're
thinking about adding online messaging.

HOST:

How, nice. George!

GEORGE:

We track the status of every job, from arrival to shipping.
And we're so confident of our ability to deliver on-time, we
offer our customers the opportunity to view the status of
their job via the internet.

HOST:

Do you indeed? George you are The Strongest link!

Scene 5: QUESTION 2

HOST:

Now George, you were the strongest link, Manny you fell
miserably behind and Sam - a pathetic last place.
Contestants, Growing volume and the demand for personalization
have made it more difficult to maintain integrity and operate
efficiently. How can you ensure quality of output while
improving your operations? Sam!

SAM:

Well, we work around the clock to make up for our mistakes.

HOST:

Manny!

MANNY: (looks proud)

We've hired a small army of people to perform manual quality checks regularly. When they all show up, we really don't miss that many…of course, it does slow down our processing a little.

HOST:

George!

GEORGE:

First of all, our systems are faster and more efficient than ever, allowing us to do more with fewer resources. In addition, we've automated mail piece tracking and integrity, eliminating manual quality checks - These steps have made it possible to increase production and quality at the same time, without increasing production costs.

HOST:

George, you are correct.

Manny and Sam, you *might* qualify for the toddler version of our game.

Scene 7: QUESTION 3

HOST:

Contestants, speaking of eliminating quality problems, it is now time for our elimination round. That is when we do everyone a favor and send one of you home.

The question is, how can you be sure you are running your operations as cost efficiently and profitably as possible?

Sam!

SAM:

Pass.

HOST:

Manny!

MANNY: (sarcastic and confused)

We use the clear and accurate data from the forms that our operators fill out, then we take the square footage of our operation center times pi and divide that by our CEO's daily caloric intake to determine the derivative of the….(cut off by Host)

HOST: (interrupts)

Manny you frighten me.   George!

GEORGE:

We stay profitable through real-time tracking, efficient job scheduling and accurate, up to the minute job costing. This is all automated for us and available at the touch of a button.

HOST:

You are correct. I wish I could say the same for your competitors.

Scene 9: THROW OFF SAM

HOST:

The moment of truth has arrived. Sam, to put it kindly, you were not the Strongest Link. In fact you've set a new low for performance on this show. I am pleased you are good at something.

Goodbye.

Scene 9a: SAM'S CONFESSION

SAM:

You know, I guess I'm not a very good production manager. I need a new career. Maybe I'll become a game show host.

Scene 10: QUESTION 4

HOST:

George and Manny. A duo yes, but not so dynamic. This is our final question. Contestants, As a production manager, how do you manage the integration of all the technologies required to

meet the challenges of a high volume automated document
factory? Manny!

MANNY:

Well, I'm personally responsible for all of our technology
integration. I find it very simple, all technology is
basically the same. Once you find the gizmo that connects the
whatsit valve, you pretty much have it licked…unless of
course, it has a…(cut off by host)

HOST:

(looks disgusted with Manny, then turns)

George!

GEORGE:

I know my strengths are in managing a highly complex
production environment; I don't have time to worry about
multiple vendor technology integration. I have selected a
vendor that takes care of all of that for me. They consult
with me to determine what our operations require, make
recommendations, and manage the implementation of integrated
solutions customized to our needs.

HOST:

George, you are correct.

Scene 12: GEORGE WINS

HOST:

Once again, George was the strongest link. Manny, thank you
for playing our game, but the customers have spoken. Goodbye.

George, your grasp of an efficient, flexible and profitable automated document factory has proven you are the strongest link.

GEORGE:

Thanks Gretchen.

Scene 13: AUDIENCE PARTICIPATION

HOST:

Now audience, it's you turn to play. You have been provided with a paper and pencil. Let me state this now. No chewing of the pencils.

You will be asked four questions, at the end of which we will see who truly is the strongest link. Are you ready?

The relationship with Bowe Bell and Howell continued with a few more product specific videos that sought to update the marketing library and show of some new features. One of these was for a "document factory" called the BookletMaker, an amazing mechanical behemoth that orchestrated a series of actions that transformed paper, ink, staples and a customer database into neatly sorted, ready to mail booklets. The machine was a major entry into on-demand publishing, and we were tasked with showing it in action.

A product demonstration video is a common genre in the industrial video world. In this case the video needed to promote the product online, in tradeshow presentations, and to give the sales team an easy way to demonstrate the device without paying to bring customers into the plant or worse, trying to ship a machine to them, a task that was nearly impossible. Video was the perfect medium to show something like this in action. Think of it as the crayon film for the machinery, one that captures the intricate details of the process from beginning to end.

A company specializing in supplemental medical plans located in Dallas was using a BookletMaker to create and mail thousands of subscriber information books. BBH wanted to send a small crew to shoot the machine in action and to get some customer testimonial footage. Armed with my Sony DV-Cam, an EZ Effects Jib and one trusty crew member, I set off to Texas to create a story about the machine, planning to show the process in action. It was a great chance to try and make my own Crayon Film.

Like most marketing pieces I've worked on, the BookletMaker project had well established messaging already in place. The client provided the bullet points enumerating the many benefits of the product and that's what formed the majority of the script. The plan was to create a story from showing the process with a narrator pushing the marketing points. The additional bits with the customer would be added where appropriate based on the best responses. The working script is included in the following pages along with a customer questionnaire that partly served as the basis for the interview questions.

Of all of the things that I learned on this piece, the most important one is this – a decent camera jib can save your ass. The choice to pack up and take the jib on a plane half way across the country was the smartest move that I made. I knew that I could make any shot more interesting with a nice camera move, and since we had considerable time to cover the narration required for the marketing points, using the jib allowed the camera to linger on a single shot for much longer without totally boring the audience. That was my theory at least, and I think it worked. Even on the most mundane angle of the machine, where the internal machinations were mostly hidden, there was elegance in the camerawork. This saved me immensely later in the editing suite, making the project one of the easiest I've ever cut together. One other note about the jib however, it nearly bit the tip of my index finger off when I carelessly tried to move the tripod under the weight of the camera, jib and counterweights by myself. But when striving for Crayon Film, a little pain was worth the effort.

DemandWorks Booklet Maker System

Video Script Draft 1
November 3, 2002

Narration:	Imagery:
1. Music fades in:	Fade in. DemandWorks fullscreen logo animation plays.
Quality, efficiency and flexibility are the focus in today's demanding document production environment. Producers need to respond quickly to customer demand, while offering more and more specialized and personalized documents.	Shots of document factory activities. Some abstract, some shots of Booklet Maker in action, all framed in the DemandWorks Letterbox frame.
Producers of saddle stitched booklets such as, **catalogs, 1 to 1 marketing materials, benefit booklets, annual statements, magazines, and other** stitched documents, especially understand the need for effective solutions that provide document integrity, maximum productivity, and path to the future.	Show text and examples of booklets. LIST: **prospectus booklets, marketing literature, catalogs, enrollment kits, benefit booklets, annual credit card summary statements, manuals, policies, statements, magazines, information kits**
2. Böwe Bell and Howell's DemandWorks Booklet Maker System provides the unique capabilities needed to exceed the expectations placed on modern document production environments, while leading the way to a true print on demand environment.	Wide product shot or Booklet Maker System Title fades in over bottom letterbox area, beside the DemandWorks logo: **Booklet Maker System**
3. The DemandWorks Booklet Maker System	Med and CU shots of Booklet Maker

is a solution that provides fully automated production of saddle-stitched booklets and other types of stitched documents. This system is capable of producing booklets from a variety of material formats including 1-Up and 2-Up continuous forms and/or cut sheet formats; and the system is capable of intelligently collating input from multiple paper streams, while maintaining 100% integrity. The ability to merge different print streams can reduce the cost of implementing digital color documents by as much as two thirds, depending on content.	Show feed system (whatever is available): Text: **1-Up Continuous Form** **2-Up Continuous Form** **Cut Sheet**
4. With a highly modular design, the system provides significant benefit to "Print On Demand" and traditional workflows, and can be configured with a variety of feeding, cutting, and collating modules to provide the flexibility to handle any stitched document application.	Wide shot, Text overlay: **Modularity** **Print on Demand** **And** **Traditional Workflows**
5. The Booklet Maker System improves productivity and efficiency in a number of ways. The system is designed to accept material from a variety of formats and intelligently collate and stitch documents. The document can then be half-folded and face-trimmed in-line with the collating and stitching to create high quality booklets. Automating the reading, feeding, cutting, merging, and collating of the document in-line with the stitching and half-folding maximizes the throughput of the system while eliminating manual processes typically associated with the production of booklets. The system's production	**Improved Productivity and Efficiency** Contextual shots from the Booklet maker in action. Split screen, video of document creation and text: **Automation** • **Reading** • **Feeding** • **Cutting**

capacity can reach 4,200 36 page booklets per hour. The performance and flexibility of the system allow the transition to a Print On Demand environment, which reduces the quantity of finished documents in inventory and reduces the scrap and rework due to frequent document updates. The system provides a level of automation that shortens the time to produce finished documents and enables **"Booklets On Demand"**. This minimizes operator intervention and the manual labor typically associated with booklet production, saving both time and money, and allowing faster response to customer demand.	• **Merging** • **Collating** • **Stitching** • **Half Folding** **Automation (clear other bullets)** • **Maximizes throughput** • **Eliminate manual processes** • **Reduce inventory** • **Reduce scrap and rework** **Booklets on Demand** • **Minimize labor** • **Cost saving** • **Quicker customer response**
6. By eliminating the manual collation of documents or the collation of documents based on fixed sheet count, the DemandWorks Booklet Maker System significantly decreases the probability of defects due to human error or miss-feeds. The system is equipped with a reading system on each of the inputs **(Input Reading Systems)** to allow for **variable collations for more personalized documents, matching of print streams, and material validation** (bullet these). These systems are capable of reading and decoding **OMR, OCR**, and various 1-d *(Code 128, I 2 of 5, 3 of 9)* and 2-d barcodes *(Data Matrix, Glyph, PDF 417)*. The reading system can report data on successfully completed documents and material usage. In addition, double feed detectors can be located on cut-sheet feeders for material that is difficult to	**Increased Product Quality and Integrity** Close ups of document flow through system Show reading systems sensors and if possible show actual scanning of documents and barcode examples Input Reading Systems • Variable collations for personalization • Matching of print streams • Material validation Show barcode examples and list if possible Show double feed detectors

singulate.	
Used in conjunction with high integrity control software, the reading system enables automated error recovery and eliminates the potential for partial or improperly collated booklets. This essential feature for personalized documents, frees the operator from constantly inspecting finished booklets for defects.	Perhaps control panel or report view here? Stills from reports may suffice
7.	
The Booklet Maker System can be in-line or near-line integrated upstream with the digital printers and/or downstream with various finishing devices such as Envelope Inserters and DemandWorks Fulfillment Automation ~~System~~ Solutions. This can result in additional cost savings from the elimination of material handling and storage between the printing and finishing operations. An additional benefit is the reduction of overall cycle time by eliminating steps in the production process – furthering the goal of achieving a true on-demand environment.	Wide shot of system Use stills if we have examples of several configs, or text: **In-line or near-line configuration with** • **Upstream digital printers** • **Downstream finishing devices** • **Inserters** • **Modular Stuffers** • **DemandWorks Fulfillment Automation System**
8.	
For organizations that are interested in a more attractive and economical alternative to pocket folders, binders or other types of unbound information for their finishing environment, Böwe Bell and Howell has the solution, the DemandWorks™ Booklet Making and Perfect Binding Systems.	Multi-image composite showing the Booklet Maker in action End on the DemandWorks Logo Fade out.

Bell & Howell Case Study Information
Customer Questionnaire

* Please provide as much detail as possible. *

Full company name:
Location (city & state):

Your name:
Your title:
Your phone:
Your e-mail:

How long has your company been in operation?

What products/services does your organization offer?

What prompted the decision to purchase [service/product/solution]? Was it a to improve customer service, an application requirement, an internal initiative, an infrastructure upgrade, etc.? Please explain.

How did you become aware of [service/product/solution]?

Please describe the investigation/selection process your organization went through to address your situation?

Why did you choose Bell & Howell's solution over other competitors?

How is [service/product/solution] meeting your expectations?

How are you using [product/solution] capabilities to better serve your customers?

What monetary and productivity gains have you realized by using [service/product/solution]?

Are you using [service/product/solution] for applications other than what is was purchased for?

How has Bell& Howell supported you since you began using [service/product/solution]?

What separates Bell & Howell from other vendors you have dealt with?

Any additional comments on [service/product/solution] and/or Bell & Howell.

Chapter 12: Demand Works One – Paper Wrapper

Another Bowe Bell & Howell project was for the DemandWorks One Paper Wrapper, a complex machine designed for large business mailers. The challenge was once again to make a series of mechanical shots flow and seem sexy. The approach to scripting the piece was to take the existing marketing bullet points and footage from the machine's operation and combine it into an interesting flow. Included here are the features of the product that provided most of the script content. The trick with a piece like this is to say as little as needed and show as much as possible. When it was determined that a large amount of information was required, we slipped in some onscreen text bullets to reinforce the narration and live action shots.

As a gadget lover by nature, these projects were a joy to create. The mechanisms alone were so fascinating and the transformative process so mesmerizing, it was very easy to choose the camera angles and set up scenes that flowed effortlessly.

The marketing materials contained some very specific technical details that to a layman meant very little. But since the audience for this video was a very informed sub-set of buyers, we tried our best to work in all of the sext details. You can see from the list below how we worked as much of the content into the final script.

BULLETS FOR VIDEO OF DEMAND WORKS ONE

AS 00:

Main drive motor

SHUTTLE FEEDER:

Up to 400 cycles per minute

Photocell for no product feed detect

Mechanical lift bar for clearing jams quickly

Feeder side lifts to give access for clearing product out of hopper

Mount position for independently powered first page opener

A4 00:

ROTARY DRUM FEEDERS (A14b):

Feeder motions by box cam (no springs)

Each feeder requires only 1/4HP to run

Capable of 400 cycles per minute

Products up to 12" x 15" on standard system

Products up to 14" x 15" on wide version for newspapers

One page up to 3/8" product thickness

Up to ½" product thickness for newspaper systems

Feeder detects no feed and double feed of product

Mount position can be provided for first page opener on any feeder

Feeder can be turned 90° in less than one minute

1.   Release handle allows moving feeder on drive shaft
2.   Turning of feeder requires no additional infeed length
3.   Mechanical lift bar
4.   Conical gear feeder mount allows you to turn it from top mount to side mount or vice versa

Possible to feed pieces from folded edge and/or open edge using unique SEP1 device

Selective feeding available

Ink Jet print-heads can be positioned after any feeder for personalization of a piece

INFEED LINE:

Flighted conveyor with one or two pusher lugs for product control

Capable of either inline (product coming from saddlestitcher, perfect binder, overhead gripper conveyor, etc.) and/or offline operation

Inline Wrapper systems can have our A.R.C. self-slowing device to allow empty flights to pass through the wrapper without making a package

Mount position before the wrapper for paper labeler or ink jet printer

Side guides width changed using a simple crankwheel

Modular design makes expansion of system as easy as plugging a new section into the line

Plug-in positions can be provided to accommodate bringing Autoloaders up to any feeder on the line

DEMAND WORKS ONE wrapper:

Wrapper has both film and paper packaging capability

Print registration system for both paper and film

InkJet print-head can be positioned beneath the machine as well as before and/or after the wrapper

Changeover from film to paper or vice versa within 15 – 20 minutes

Double brushless Servo-motors for precise electronic control on:
        Drive belt through wrapper
        Rotary cutter for paper enveloping
        Hot knife cut-off blade for film wrapping
        Paper/Film side mounted unwinder (R3P)

Allen/Bradley PLC

Swing-arm control panel

Finished packages from single page to 1"H

Film only machines up to 3"H packs

PAPER:

Rotary Cutting Blade for paper capable of production speeds up to 20,000/hr

Low temperature hot melt glue applied by proprietary mechanism on longitudinal and cross seal

Rotary cutter cuts through the cross glue line creating a clean edge on the finished envelope (no lip left behind)

FILM:

Hot knife cut-off blade for film moves along with the package by means of a special mechanical cam mechanism

Production speeds up to 14,000/hr

Unique longitudinal seal block electronically controlled for precise temperature control

PAPER/FILM UNWINDER (R3P):

Up to 40"O.D. paper rolls

Up to 23"O.D. film rolls

Hydraulic lift mechanism for paper/film rolls

Film only versions of unwinders also available

Unwind matches the speed of wrapper – no tension through wrapper

GATHERING CONVEYOR (RA5):

Takes product either inline with the system or at right angle to the system

Counter with product offset pusher can be added for ZipCode sortation

Demand Works also has line of high speed stackers

⁑ DemandWorks Film-
and Paper-Wrapping

Marketing Video Script
Draft 6

October 10, 2002

Audio	Video
1. You may not be able to judge a book by its cover, but the outside of your direct mailpiece may be more influential than you think. Today billers, direct mailers and other producers of high-volume mail have a new efficient and customizable alternative to traditional envelopes. An alternative that adds a new layer of eye catching personalization to standard communications such as bills and advertising campaigns.	Fade-In: Graphic sequence involves a number of mailpiece examples, both boring and dynamic – illustrating the effectiveness of customized and personalized mailpieces. Background may include abstract mailpiece machinery shots for a little flair. Sequence likely an After Effects composite
2. With the fastest processing speeds available on the market, Bell and Howell's DemandWorks Film and Paper-Wrapping Systems enable companies to produce higher-quality and more cost-effective mailpieces.	Best of the best b-roll of product in a short montage Keywords float: *higher-quality* *cost-effective*
3. Using Paper or Film Wrap to envelop mailpiece enclosures in a secure continuous process the DemandWorks Patented Film and Paper-Wrapping Systems allow companies to create customizable mailpieces in real time. This eliminates the cost and space	Show the equipment in action – wrapping a nice example of personalized mailpiece. Follow a series of pieces through the process. Maybe have an operator pick one up at the end as if inspecting it – Camera gets a good look. Keywords float: *Eliminate Cost and free up floorspace* *Personalization*

requirements associated with printing and storing pre-printed envelopes while creating new avenues of personalization.	
4. These include targeted marketing messages, company logos, and customized designs. Since each enclosure is enveloped one at a time, the DemandWorks Film and Paper-Wrapping Systems help to increase an organization's overall document efficiency, integrity and accuracy.	Wide on equipment in operation, mutes to a duo tone – fades into background. Examples of mailpieces come forward with keyword. Keywords: ***Targeting Marketing Messages*** ***Logos*** ***Customized Designs*** Show close up of machinery in action – wraps, one at a time. (Maybe a "slowmo" effecting a composited window) ***Efficiency*** ***Integrity*** ***Accuracy*** Shot of operator examining the flow of the machinery
5. The DemandWorks Film and Paper-Wrapping Systems are available in the following models: DemandWorks 2500, which features Film-Wrapping speed of 15,000 pieces per hour. DemandWorks 3000, with the Film-Wrapping speed of 21,000 pieces per hour an. And DemandWorks One, which features Paper-Wrapping speed of 20,000 pieces per hour, and Film-Wrapping speed of 15,000 pieces per hour.	Background is muted video, Foreground features overlay of each model, ***text title and wrapping speed information***

6. Designed with modularity in mind, these systems allow for maximum flexibility and easy installation in both continuous and stop-motion environments. Take a look at some of the system components and features.	Live action, or photo/graphic animation showing different configurations of Systems Keyword: ***Modularity*** ***Flexibility***
7. SHUTTLE FEEDER SCENE: The DemandWorks Paper and Film Wrapping System can have either a shuttle feeder or a rotary drum feeder, both capable of up to 400 cycles per minute. The shuttle feeder features a photocell sensor for no product feed detection and the rotary drum feeder integrates a caliber device for double feeder detection and a photocell for no product feed detection. The shuttle feeder includes a mechanical lift bar for quick clearing of product jams, and the feeder side lifts provide easy access to product in the hopper. A mount position for an independently powered first page opener is also available.	Wide and medium shot of shuttle feeder CU move into photocell Show jam being cleared Med shot of feeder operating
8. ROTARY DRUM FEEDERS SCENE: To provide flexibility for a wide range of applications, the ROTARY DRUM FEEDER features a singulating disk, which allows the feeding of pieces from either open or folded edge at speeds up to 400 cycles per minute. The feeder operates by box cam, requiring no springs and requires only ¼ horse-power for operation.	Med and inside cu of the feeder

The Rotary Drum Feeder can be easily adjusted to different product with maximum size of up to 12 by 15 inches with thickness up to 3/8 of an inch on the standard system and 14 by 15 inches and ½ of an inch thickness on the unique newspaper system.	Show adjustment of product feed Wider image mute as bg and show text of sizes in foreground
For flexibility and convenience, the feeder can be turned ninety degrees for side feeding in less than one minute without requiring additional infeed length.	Cu's of sensors or wider of feeder in operation Sequence that shows the rotation of feeder
Employing the unique SEP1 device, the feeder makes it possible to feed pieces from the folded edge and open edge. For increased personalization, the feeder supports selective feeding, and Ink Jet print-heads can be positioned after any feeder.	Show the Singulating disk here
9. Infeed line The DemandWorks Paper and Film Wrapping System's Infeed line consists of a flighted conveyor with one or two pusher lugs for product control.	Show med move down inline feed
The system is capable of offline operation, or inline operation with systems such as the Saddlesticher, Perfect Binder, or an overhead griper (is this griper or gripper?) conveyor. And the system's modular design makes expansion as easy as plugging a new section into the line.	Wide image as bg Text **Compatibility with:** **Saddlesticher** **Perfect Binder** **overhead griper (gripper?) conveyor** **Etc.**
To ensure reliability, efficiency and mailpiece integrity, Inline Wrapper systems feature the optional A.R.C. self-slowing device to allow empty flights to pass through the wrapper without making a package. This also maximizes production speed and net throughput.	Text over med moving shot. "A.R.C. Gap Recovery System"

Offering a great deal of flexibility, the system features a mount position before the wrapper for a paper labeler and/or an InkJet printer.	Show InkJet mount area,
For varied product sizes, the operator can easily change the side guides width using a simple crank wheel.	show side guide sequence
10. Wrapper DemandWorks offers systems with both film and paper packaging capabilities. Optional co-existing paper cutters and film sealers allow for fast, efficient changeover between paper and film.	Wide shot of system Med showing both types of cutters
For increased personalization options, the print registration system for controlling package length repeat, can be combined with InkJet print-heads for printing personalized messages or mailing addresses. These heads can be positioned after a feeder, before and or after the wrapper, or even below the wrapper on the film unwind.	Cu of registration sensors Move on print head Motor shot Cu of cutters working
The system uses double brushless servo-motors to ensure precise electronic control for the drive belt through the wrapper, the rotary paper cutter, the hot knife cut-off blade for film wrapping, and the paper/film unwinder.	Wide of unwinder Med of PLC Swing arm pulled over by Harry
At the heart of the system's electronics is the Allen/Bradley PLC, which provides the precision and reliability required for the most complex operations. The convenient swing-arm control panel provides the operator easy access to system functions.	
11. Paper Operations: In paper wrapping operations, low temperature hot-melt glue is applied to longitudinal and cross seal to ensure high quality mailpiece creation	Show glue application Product flowing

The rotary cutting blade, which is capable of production speeds up to 20,000 pieces per hour, cuts through the cross glue line to create a clean edge on the finished envelope.	CU on rotary blade in action
Paper wrapping systems can support finished packages with as little as a single page, to thicknesses up to 1 inch.	Show product on conveyor – different thickness
12. FILM: For film operations, the system employs an electronically monitored longitudinal seal block for precise temperature control.	CU on sealer
To ensure precise cuts and effective seals, the hot knife cut-off blade moves with the package by means of a special cam mechanism. Production speeds for film wrapping can reach up to 15,000 pieces per hour.	Show knife, tilt down to cam Super text
Optional dual cross sealers for film applications maximize the systems production speed and reliability while delivering up to 21,000 pieces per hour.	

13. PAPER/FILM UNWINDER: The Demandworks Paper and Film Wrapping System's paper/film unwinder can accommodate up to forty-seven inch outside-diameter paper rolls, and up to 23 inch outside diameter film rolls. For easy loading and unloading, the unwinder incorporates a hydraulic lift mechanism. To eliminate tension through the wrapper, the unwind speed matches the speed of the wrapper. For personalization, an InkJet print-head can be positioned beneath the machine as well as before and/or after the wrapper.	Move on the unloader **Work out text super for this sequence Show wide of lift Move from paper wind at base over to inkjet head CU on inkjet head
14. GATHERING CONVEYOR: The Gathering Conveyor works either inline with the system or at a right angle to transport finished product. For Zip Code sortation, a counter with a product offset pusher can be added to the system. DemandWorks also features a line of high speed stackers.	Move to conveyor
8. Wrap up DemandWorks Film and Paper-Wrapping Systems. For unmatched flexibility, efficiency, and reliability, look no further than Bell and Howell.	Highlight reel of b-roll,etc. End on Bell & Howell Logo

Chapter 13: BIPS
Return of the racing metaphor

One additional project for Bowe Bell and Howell came after VisionFactory dissolved. The project was for a tradeshow presentation at a show called XPLOR 2003. The subject was an automated changeover system for BBH's on-demand printing solution called "BIPS" - BÖWE Intelligent Productivity System.

As with previous projects we had some existing marketing footage and animations, key bullet points, and we shot some new product shots. But since this presentation needed a hook for the tradeshow audience, we developed the idea of "The Race", a series of vignettes pitting a BBH branded racecare against three generic competitors. Returning to the speed and performance themes that were so successful with the early Internet Thruway video, this NASCAR based metaphor was a perfect way to brand not only the video, but the handouts and the booth design for the show.

I at this point in my career, I had moved from Research Triangle Park to Asheville, NC and had started my own business. Fortunately I had maintained a connection with the client and with the graphic designer from VisionFactory, Meri Kotlas. For this project Meri provided the graphic design and I turned to a local animator to create the racing animations to use in the piece. The budget wasn't too high, but everyone contributed stellar work nonetheless.

This piece was one of many where I returned to the role of producer as well as director and screenwriter. The many years at VisionFactory had placed me in all of these roles in differing degrees on hundreds of projects. Now, with my own company, that experience was incredibly valuable in turning around a project quickly while managing other resources and delivering on client expectations.

A.   Title Sequence

Fade in:

COMPOSITE ANIMATION – RACING IMAGERY AND **Böwe Bell & Howell** imagery form a multi-paneled image as music mixes up

PROGRAM TITLE

"Böwe Bell & Howell, Leading the Pack"

Swooshes over the image.

B.   Intro – "The Race"

The screen transitions to a Letterboxed frame featuring Racing image overlays on the top and bottom bars and the Böwe Bell & Howell Logo in the upper left. The bottom bar of the screen serves as a "bullet and title" area.

The Title "**THE RACE**" Swoops onto the screen and dissolves\

A wide shot of the Turbo 22 Configuration fills the letterboxed area.

NARRATOR:

The race to meet customer demand is on. Printing and mailing centers are experiencing increasing volumes and shorter cycle times. Service providers face growing customer pressure for varying document formats and sizes, higher levels of personalization and the need for accurate, continuous tracking.

To meet these challenges, Böwe Bell & Howell introduces the BIPS Turbo22 – the next level of flexibility, speed and performance for inserting systems. By combining the industry-leading **Turbo22** inserter and the revolutionary new **BIPS** changeover system, Böwe Bell & Howell is setting the pace with increased productivity, maximum repeatability and easy operation.

Get ready to leave your competition in the dust!

A series of overlapped dissolves of slightly moving footage explore the key features of the machine, its components and its many control systems.

C. Car Animation Transition – "The Ride – Turbo 22 Components"
FULL SCREEN ANIMATION - RACETRACK - CAR

A NASCAR car with BBH and BIPS logos mapped in various places is being led by the camera as it pulls down the track.

The engine sound is loud and consistent here.

The title fades up - "The Ride – Turbo 22 Components "

Notes: Clip Length – 10 sec.

Camera moving just ahead of lead car

Potential keywords to map on track wall – "Modularity" "Efficiency"

D. Component features
This segment concentrates on the very high level features of the Components that make up the Vanguard Config. This is done though a sequence of animated push-in's on a wireframed model of the complete system. For instance:

380Stream Cutter

The camera arcs around the wireframed model of the System, as it moves toward the 380Stream Cutter Module. While approaching the module, the textures and colors form, "un-wireframing" only that module. The camera settles to a stop as the module takes the focus of the frame.

This technique will be used on the following areas of the model:

1. 380Stream Cutter
2. The Accufold with the Merger, Assembly Station and Folder
3. Sequencer
4. Assembly station
5. Enclosure feeder
6. Inserting station
7. Envelope Feeder

Split screen approach:

For instances where video details are required - animation will recede into the left third of the Letterbox area and the remaining 2/3 screen will be used for the video content.

This sequence repeats for the major component sections of the System.

NARRATOR:

The Turbo22 is truly a high-performance machine, offering unmatched ease of operation and flexibility that are due to Böwe Bell & Howell's seamless integration of input modules.

In any race, time spent on Pit Row is basically lost time. That's why we've minimized the amount of operator involvement required by the Turbo22. With state-of-the-art input modules, barcode camera technology and complete mailpiece tracking, the BIPS Turbo22 provides the ultimate in document integrity with minimal effort.

The 590 Speed sheet feeder and 380 STREAM cutting system get the Turbo22 off to a fast start. Clocking in at over 49,000 forms per hour, these systems make the Turbo 22 the highest performance, two-channel inserting system available.

For Flexible handling of documents, Böwe Bell & Howell's Accufold system accommodates 1-up or 2-up forms. Capable of merging east to west or west to eas, and assembling groups in A-Z or Z-A sequence based on job specs, the Accufold system can create half-fold with up to 12 sheets in a single group and tri-folds with up to 8 sheets.

The Sequencer supports varying format heights and includes on edge paper transport capability, orienting documents from the horizontal plane to vertical for precision handling at top rated speeds.

The flexibility continues at the Assembly Station where the folded documents from separate input streams are intelligently matched and then merged in A-Z or Z-A sequence with utmost integrity.

At the inserting station, **the BIPS Turbo22 kicks into high gear, leading the pack** with 22,000 cycles per hour. The inserter and integrated envelope feeder process a variety of formats including DL, #10, 6x9, and C5, making it the ideal solution for a demanding production schedule.

Together, these **finely tuned technologies** combine to create **a winning machine** for you and your customers.

E.   Car Animation Transition - BIMAS

FULL SCREEN ANIMATION – THE BBH car comes toward the camera and wipes the screen revealing the title:

"BIMAS – Precision Control"

F.   BIMAS - Handshake Technologies

The screen transitions to the Letterboxed frame. The bullet area displays "BIMAS - Böwe Bell & Howell Integrated Mailcenter Automation System"

NOTE: THIS SEQUENCE MAY RELY HEAVILY ON GRAPHICS TO CONVEY SOME OF THE CONTENT.

BICOS is heavily reliant on screenshots to show features. Also there is an MPEG animation that may be usable.

ANV - Video content will be acquired to show the hardware elements of the ANV system including the sensors, plus examples of the Bar-coding or other image-based controls elements.

NARRATOR:

Precision and control make all of the difference in the race to meet customer demand. Böwe Bell & Howell's Integrated Mailcenter Automation System, or BIMAS, gives you the **performance tools** you need to finish out on top.

Böwe Bell & Howell's Handshake Technology digitally marks every item as it enters the system. Integrated optical sensors and timers help track the movement of all documents, enclosures and envelopes, while the BICOS user interface monitors material tracking and matching.

Optional Account Number Verification Software, or ANV, provides a detailed audit report of all documents processed by the system. In the event of errors, the system will stop or automatically divert the package in question, while recording the errors in a reprint file.

BIMAS is the key for centralizing and monitoring all production data in a multi-system environment. It provides real-time production statistics and audit reports to help maintain the highest level of integrity in any document factory.

G.   Car Animation Transition – BIPS
FULL SCREEN ANIMATION - RACETRACK - PIT AREA – 10 Seconds

High up, just in front of the Lead car's Pit Area, the camera captures the car as it pulls onto pit row and screeches to a stop inches from the Böwe Bell & Howell Placard at the front of the Pit area. As this is happening, the camera arcs down closer to fill the frame with the car.

NARRATOR:

Let's face it. Changeovers can be the pits. The entire production schedule can come crashing to a screeching halt due to a simple application format or size change.

THE CAR SLIDES INTO THE PIT.

NARRATOR (cont.)

That's why Böwe Bell & Howell developed BIPS, a high-octane solution to automating job changeovers..

H.   BIPS
The screen dissolves from the full screen car to a model of the Vanguard Configuration (all components) and the letterbox frames slide into place from top and bottom.

The title and logo for "BIPS - BÖWE Intelligent Productivity System" appears in the bullet area. Can't we just use the BIPS logo...leave off Böwe etc

The model recedes to the left 1/3 of the screen as video of the machine's automatic adjustment process fills the other 2/3. This includes mechanical changeovers and screenshots.

The model turns to wireframe and highlights each area contextually (Production note - this can be done though a series of stills)

The sounds of a pit crew can be heard throughout this sequence.

> NARRATOR:
>
> The Böwe Intelligent Productivity System, or BIPS, is a revolutionary approach to job changeover aimed at increasing productivity, maximizing repeatability and ensuring simple operation.
>
> With BIPS, the operator can change over the inserting system for a new application in just a few minutes with no mechanical intervention. Form sizes, fold types, assembling sequences and envelope sizes are just a few examples of the many job parameters that can be programmed into the BICOS user interface. These settings control the motor-driven changeover of the system. This dramatically reduces job setup times since the job parameters are stored in the system for simple retrieval in the future.
>
> A conventional job changeover can take anywhere from 20 to 30 minutes. With BIPS, you're back on track in just two minutes – potentially gaining up to 10,000 envelopes in production performance.
>
> BIPS orchestrates the changeover process, no matter how complex it may be. Once the optimized job settings have been programmed and stored, the system will set itself to those original settings whenever the job is loaded. This eliminates dial-in periods, which translates into greater productivity and efficiency – an all-around winning combination.

Change-over sequence video cuts:

- Cutter

- Merger
- Assembly Station
- Folding module
- Sequencer
- Insert Assembly station
- Collating track
- Inserting station
- Envelope transport

I.   **WRAP-UP-Winning the Race**

FULL SCREEN ANIMATION - RACETRACK FINISH LINE – 20 Sec

Camera looks across the finish line toward the approaching cars. There is a grandstand as well as a large Jumbo Tron screen just over the grandstand to the left of the track. This will display the Three Points:

"   Increased Productivity

"   Maximum Repeatability

"   Easiest Operation

And appropriate logo.

NARRATOR:

Increased Productivity, Maximum Repeatability and Easy Operation

The Turbo22 with BIPS . . . just another way Böwe Bell & Howell is helping you win the race for your customers.

See it in action here at Xplor 2003.

The Cars approach the finish line and the BBH car is the clear winner, crossing the line and passing through the frame. The other cars don't even make the line before the image Fades Out.

BBH LOGO TREATMENT FADES UP and loops.

Stills from the BBH BIPS project.

Chapter 14: CipherOptics
Ever see those Mac Guy, PC Guy Commercials?

CipherOptics was a company that provided software for network encryption. They had developed a flexible, cost-effective solution that traditionally was the domain of router companies. Their product allowed sensitive data to be shared securely over the network – a godsend to businesses like hospitals that had to comply with strict regulations.

My former VisionFactory boss referred the marketing team from CipherOptics to me to produce a series of spots that they had been wanting to do for a while. Their concept was to take the Mac Guy and PC Guy concept that had been done so brilliantly by Apple and create a similar set of guys to pitch the benefits of their security software. Hence, Router Guy and Solutions Guy were born.

The question of homage or parody came up again with this project, and I'm not sure if I know which end we came down on. I just know that the client had a vision and a budget so we jumped in to see what we could create. There were four initial scripts roughed out by the client and I took their material as a starting point as I tried to work out the problems we'd face. We knew we wanted humor and we wanted to explain some specific features of a normally hard to understand set of products. Solutions Guy represented CipherOptics. He was to be the answer to all of the problems brought up by Router Guy, the inflexible, somewhat bumbling character. This framework was done to perfection for Apple by John Hodgman and Jason Long, so I knew I'd have to be very creative with how I wrote the pieces and how I'd eventually cast the two characters.

While writing the scripts, I decided that each of the eventual five pieces would need to remain brief. If they were to work at all they'd have to hold the audience for a moment and then quickly deliver a punch line. For the casting I took a bit of a chance and called upon two friends, Tom Maxwell of the band The Squirrel Nut Zippers, and another musician friend, Billy Sugarfix. The two contrasted well, and I knew that both understood comedy. Since the budget was modest, I knew that working with folks I'd worked with before would help us get the most from the two scheduled shooting days. One additional role was cast with Meredith Sause who to my great benefit helped out as the production manager for the shoot.

The CipherOptics pieces were done as metaphors. We decided that the more simple the device to make the point, the better, settling on things like a series of crying babies to represent government regulatory agencies, Jenga games to represent network stability, a huge stack of paper to show complexity, etc. It was all very playful and a direct contrast to the normal tech jargon that would be employed to discuss digital encryption software. Having a client that was willing to take these chances was very freeing, and the project turned out to be great fun to shoot and edit.

Following are the documents I provided to the actors along with the five scripts for the project.

CipherOptics Viral Video Spots Scripts

Here are the five scripts for the CipherOptics Project. Hopefully there will not be significant changes before the shoot.

The concept was the client's idea to take the MAC guy/ PC Guy commercials and apply them to their product which is an Internet, Networking Security software product. Traditionally security is achieved through encryption introduced through the routers of a network. This requires code to be added to the all of the routers in the network. Router Guy represents this method – it is cumbersome, complex, and not very flexible. Solutions Guy represents the CipherOptics product which uses software to do this much more effectively.

So Router Guy is a bit set in his ways – I imagine a bit nerdy and convinced his way is the way to go. Of course it always goes wrong in our examples.

Solutions Guy is the more relaxed, cool of the two. His solution is always simple. His reactions to Router Guy's nervous fumbling will be key to making the spots work.

Although the content might seem a bit cryptic to a standard audience, the client's target audience – mainly these network security guys are very focused on the things each spot focuses on. So I hope the humor works for them while making points about the product.

With two days in the studio I think we'll make it through these without any trouble. I think the approach will be to take them one at a time, rehearse and then shoot before moving to the next. They are short enough that I think we'll find our groove pretty quickly.

I'm looking forward to working with you.

Steve

White screen – the words "Square Pegs" fades up
Light music mixes in

Dissolve to:

White Set - Router Guy and Solutions Guy

are standing side-by-side behind a table Before each is a small wooden, child's shapes game made up of square, triangle, rectangle and circle shaped holes and four handled pieces beside. The Router Guy board is labeled – "ROUTER", Solutions Guy's –"CipherEngine"

Behind them in the center is a movie screen on a stand.

> Narrator (off-screen)
> Let's say you are in charge of protecting my
> company's information on this type of network.

The screen shows Square with MPLS network

> Solutions Guy
> You can solve that problem with CipherEngine.

He places a square piece into the square hole.

> Router Guy
> You can solve that problem in the router too.

He places a square piece into the square hole.

> Narrator
> OK, but what if you have this type of network,
> or this, or this?

The screen shows circle, rectangle, and triangle labeled as VPLS, Metro Ethernet, Hybrid.

> Solutions Guy
> Yes, yes and yes.

He places the three other pieces in their proper holes.

                        Router Guy
            Umm….

He tries to put square peg into round hole.

                        Narrator
            Router Guy, I don't think that really fits.

                        Router Guy
                  (struggling to shove peg in)
            Gimme a sec

            .

                        Solutions Guy
            Yeah, I don't think that's going to work.

Router guy is looking at all of his pieces, all squares.

                        Router Guy
            You know what? I have a solution

                        Narrator
            Really?

Router guy reaches under the table and produced a board with four square holes.

                        Router Guy
            Yeah, you just need to buy one of these.

Flip to End Screen:

Secure Information Sharing over *any* network:

Powered by CipherEngine

Jenga
(aka "Router's Block")

White screen – the word "Security Jenga" fades up
Light music mixes in

Dissolve to:

White Set - Router Guy and Solutions Guy

are standing side-by-side behind a table. They are facing the camera. Before each of them is a rectangle of small wooden "Jenga" blocks. (These may be in a vertical tower like the game, or more cleverly shaped like a router. In this configuration of the blocks, the word ROUTER is clear on the side of the blocks.)

> Narrator (off-screen)
> Let's say you are in charge of protecting my company's
> information on the network.

> Router Guy
> You can solve that problem in the router.
> (begins swapping blocks)
> You just need to make some minor changes
> (begins talking to himself)

Router guy slides a block out and begins to build a less stable block pile. Repeats.

Solutions guy glances over at the activity then looks back to camera.

> Solutions Guy
> There's a better way to do this

Close up on Solutions Guy as he places a transparent box over his set of blocks. He looks up and smiles.

Wider - Router guy continues to mumble and make changes. His block tower looks impossibly complex.

> Narrator
> Uh,… that looks a little complicated. Won't
> that affect the routers performance?

                              Router Guy
                    Oh no. These things are great.

He continues to fine tune his block sculpture.

                              Narrator
                    But that doesn't look very stable

                              Router Guy
                    It's fine really.

                              Narrator
                    But won't any network stress or application
                    use cause you problems?

                              Router Guy
                    Oh no these things are inextricable .
                         (pauses, he is about to sneeze)
                    Excuse me.

Router guy takes a handkerchief from his pocket and sneezes into it. His router tower
tumbles on cue. He looks down and without missing a best, looks back up.

                              Router Guy
                    We could always buy a bigger router.

Flip to End Screen:

Secure Information Sharing with the network you already have:

Powered by CipherEngine

Papers (aka Simplicity)

White screen – the word "Simplicity" fades up
Light music mixes in

Dissolve to:

White Set - Router Guy and Solutions Guy

are standing side-by-side behind a table. They are facing the camera. Behind them in the center is a movie screen on a stand.

> Narrator
> Lets say you are in charge of protecting
> my company's information on the network.

The words "Protecting the information on the network" appear on the movie screen behind the guys. They glance to the screen.

> Router Guy
> You can solve that problem in the router:

> Solutions Guy
> There's a better way to solve the problem

> Narrator
> OK, well if my network looks like this.
> How much configuration code do I need?

Flip to diagram 1 on the screen. It is a simple network layout.

Router guy reaches out of the left of the frame and retrieves a single sheet of paper and holds it up.

> Router Guy
> Each router needs this.

Solutions Guy reaches to frame right and retrieves a single sheet and also holds it up.

> Solutions Guy
> With CipherEngine it only takes this.

Narrator
That's great, but what if my network looks like this

Flip to diagram 2 on the screen, a more complex network. The guys look and Router guy reaches out and returns with a stack of pages.

Router Guy
In that case each router needs this. (shakes his head proudly)

Solutions Guy
With CipherEngine, still just this.

Narrator
Hmm, but what if my network looks like this?

Flip to diagram 3 on the screen, an even more complex network. Router Guy looks nervously.
Router Guy
Just a second.

then walks out of frame. Solutions Guy holds up his single sheet.

Solutions Guy
Still just this.

Router Guy makes some noise off-screen as Solutions Guy looks curiously. He re-enters frame with hand truck full of papers

Router Guy
Where do you want all this?

Narrator
You know what, I don't

Flip to End Screen:

Secure Information Sharing without complexity:
Powered by CipherEngine

Compliance

White screen – the word "Compliance" fades up
Light music mixes in

Dissolve to:

White Set - Router Guy and Solutions Guy

are side by side as a series of baby bassinets are rolled into a line between them. A label on the front of each bassinet is that of an agency requiring compliance (*HIPAA, GLBA, RIPA, FFIEC, NERC*-we choose top five or find a way to have multiples on a label.). As each rolls in the *loud cries* of the babies (unseen) inside build. A total of 5 identical bassinets rest to form a perfect line between the two guys.

> Narrator (off-screen)
> We have to satisfy some pretty stringent criteria with
> the security of our network.

Router Guy looks up from the line of babies and faces the camera.

> Router Guy
> No problem.

Router Guy walks off the edge of the frame and returns with an armful of different baby item, rattlers, etc. and proceeds to perform for the babies. He is joined by three other Router guys, all performing.. The cries grow even louder.

Solutions guy looks on with a grin and a disagreeing nod.

Router guys become more frantic to no avail. Cries continue.

Solution guy steps out of frame and returns with a small music box. He winds a crank on the side. It plays "Rockabye baby…"
The cries one by one subside until the music box is the only sound.

Flip to End Screen

Compliance-Grade™ Safe Passage solutions

Powered by CipherEngine

Control

White screen – the word "Compliance" fades up
Light music mixes in

Dissolve to:

White Set - Solutions Guy is standing on the set behind a small table with a laptop. Router guy

> Narrator (off-screen)
> We need to update security for the entire network.

Router guy walks off Camera left. Solutions Guy opens his laptop. Router Guy walks into frame carrying a load of luggage and is dressed to the hilt as a tourist. Solutions Guy gives him the once over.

> Router Guy
> Cool. I'm going to get a ton of frequent flyer miles.

Solutions Guy returns focus to his laptop and clicks a couple of simple strokes on his keyboard.

> Solutions Guy
> Done.

> Router Guy
> Done? I thought he said update the entire network.

> Solutions Guy
> I just did.

> Narrator (off-screen)
> How big is your network?

Solutions Guy looks at Router Guy

> Solutions Guy
> Same as his.

Flip to End Screen

Universal Access, Centralized Control

Powered by CipherEngine

Chapter 15: HP Cooltown and Atlanta Business Center
Two men, a dolly and a Jib

There were many similarities between the humble beginning of HP and VisionFactory. Like HP, VisionFactory was literally started in a garage. Our first edit suites and After Effects machines resided in a small out building at the co-owners house in Durham, NC. It was there that I first learned how to cut on a Media 100 non-linear editing system. It was an upgrade from Adobe Premiere 1.0 on the PC – the system that I cut my 35mm feature film "Immortal" on (fodder for a different book altogether). Unlike VisionFacotry however, HP grew over 40 years to be a computing powerhouse.

Carly Fiorina was the dynamic CEO of HP during the late 1990's when we pitched a customer center concept called CoolTown. Like our other briefing center work, CoolTown was an experiential space that exploited networked technologies and fresh architectural approaches. CoolTown also featured the concept of a Living Lab – a reconfigurable space that would allow customers to simulate networks, and co-create products with HP. The concept was very exciting, and like other pitches we had prepared, the CoolTown project produced some slick marketing videos as well as a detailed project spec. The timing for CoolTown wasn't ideal. It was a time in the late 90's that corporate marketing began to take a hit, and the dollars and interest for the project quickly succumbed to budget constraints and a weakening market.

CoolTown was to be based at HP's headquarters in Silicon Valley. When the project fizzled we were disappointed, but all of the work eventually led to a smaller project for a Business Networking Center based in Atlanta, Georgia. The center featured secure severs buried deep in the basement of a large skyscraper which also housed hundreds of HP networking experts and IT business consultants.

The project called for the creation of several video vignettes focusing on various parts of the operation. The budget was small and we had only one day to shoot all of the footage onsite. Armed with a doorway dolly, EZ-FX jib and an assistant I crammed a very full day shooting everything interesting in site. The best lesson from a shoot like this is that a jib yields long gliding shots that can cover periods of narration when there is nothing left to cut to. With a project like this, getting enough coverage is essential, so we shot a variety of angles at each location within the building and pulled in as many extras as we could from the staff. Fortunately we were given free reign from the client during the shoot.

Knowing that some of the content wouldn't have corresponding video footage, the script and resulting production used many photographs and some graphics provided by the client. The project was an exercise in making things work, and though it was tricky at times to fill the visuals, I'm proud of the final product, especially based on the small budget.

Fade In:

BRAND BARRAGE - ANIMATION

A series of still images of
HP products, services
personnel, and end users
animate onscreen into the
four panels of the HP
presentation brand standard.
Alternating with this image
assault is a series of text
quotes also animating
forward.   These quotes
include:

"We strive to be easily
accessible and highly
responsive."

"Technical excellence
unsurpassed in the industry"

"Helping our customers
succeed is the ultimate
success."

"Treating our customers with
courtesy, respect, and
professionalism"

The HP Services Standard
logo comes to the forefront.

"Speed, Power and Passion –
the HP Services Standard"

The opening is over in about
45 seconds.

Screen dips to black.

MUSIC PIPES UP

IT IS A COMBINATION OF
HIGH TECH MUSIC AND
DRIVING PERCUSSION.   THE
MUSIC'S ENERGY COMPLIMENTS
THE ANIMATION OF TEXT AND
IMAGES.

MUSIC PEAKS AND GOES QUIET

CUSTOMER RESPONSES

This section focuses on customer testimonial soundbites. If customer soundbites are appropriate for other sections of the script, they will be used there also.

The first customer testimonial clip appears here.

Marty Gettman, Director of Support Services - McKesson

LIGHT MUSIC BED PLAYS AGAINST TESTIMONIALS.

MARTY GETTMAN

TALKS ABOUT HIS EXPERIENCE

RELYING ON HP SERVICES.

Other customer clips may appear here.

AWARDS MONTAGE

A graphical montage of award text plays out in on rectangle, as the identifying text for the awards displays in the other.

Imagery includes CIO Award – from WebBusiness, ASP award from The Association of Support Professionals, and The Star Award from SSPA. There are also shots of the Business 2.0 article entitled: "The Ultimate Help Desk".

CSI Survey Info will also be used here along with any customer letters

NARRATOR

AS A LEADER IN SUPPORT, HP HAS

BEEN RECOGNIZED BY THE INDUSTRY

THROUGH A SERIES OF

PUBLICATIONS AND SERVICE

AWARDS. THESE INCLUDE THE

PRESTIGIOUS 2001 STAR AWARD FOR

SERVICE EXCELLENCE FROM THE

SERVICE AND SUPPORT

PROFESSIONALS ASSOCIATION, AND

AWARDS FROM WEBBUSINESS.

highlighting hp's support.

HP'S IT RESOURCE CENTER HAS BEEN
NAMED ONE OF THE TOP TEN BEST WEB
SITES BY THE ASSOCIATION OF SUPPORT
PROFESSIONALS. THE AWARD-WINNING IT
RESOURCE CENTER PUTS OUR TRAINING AND
SUPPORT EXPERTISE ONLINE AND
OFFERS AN ACTIVE ONLINE COMMUNITY OF
OVER 740,000 MEMBERS. CUSTOMERS USE
THE IT RESCOURE CENTER TO SAVE TIME
DOWNLOADING SOFTWARE, FINDING
SOLUTIONS TO MAINTAIN THEIR
SYSTEMS AND BUILDING THEIR EXPERTISE.

HP GLOBAL SERVICES

The screen is divided into
two equally proportioned HP
rectangular containers.
During this scene one
container always features a
text message WHILE the other
features video and still
imagery. The video and text
rectangles may alternate
when appropriate.

In the right RECTANGLE is an
image of an animated globe.
This image dissolves through
a series of global imagery
including aerial shots of
metropolitan areas, map
images, people on the
streets and people doing
there jobs at HP call
centers. This montage also

Narrator

HP HAS EARNED ITS REPUTATION AS
A WORLD LEADER IN INNOVATIVE
PRODUCTS AND SERVICES. FROM OUR
DESKTOP SERVICES TO ENTERPRISE
CLASS SUPPORT, HP DELIVERS THE
PEOPLE, TOOLS, AND PROCESSES
NECESSARY TO ASSIT CUSTOMERS IN
CREATING A POWERFUL IT
INFRASTRUCTURE, COMPLETE WITH

includes a variety of
technology imagery. This
includes Computer racks,
abstract electronics imagery
and people working on
networking systems.

During this montage, the
left rectangle features a
series of keywords. These
include:

The HP Logo, HP Services,
Education,

Technology Finance,

HP Operations, Consulting

INDUSTRY-SPECIFIC APPLICATIONS,
BUSINESS PROCESSES AND
STRATEGIES THAT ARE REQUIRED
FOR END TO END SOLUTIONS.
A TRUE LEADER IN GLOBAL
SUPPORT, HP UTILIZES ITS GLOBAL
KNOWLEDGE MANAGEMENT SYSTEM TO
PROVIDE AROUND THE CLOCK,
AROUND THE WORLD SUPPORT IN
OVER ONE-HUNDRED AND TWENTY
COUNTRIES.

WITH 28,000 PROFESSIONSALS AND
35 RESPONSE CENTERS, HP
PROVIDES THE INDUSTRY STANDARD
IN HARDWARE, SOFTWARE, NETWORK,
MULTI-VENDOR, AND MULTI-
PLATFORM SUPPORT.
LEADERSHIP, RESPONSE, AND
PERFORMANCE HAVE MADE HP THE
TRUSTED ADVISOR OF CUSTOMERS
WORLDWIDE.

THE ATLANTA BUSINESS CENTER

Once again the multi-rectangle layout is used.

Perhaps a quick photo of the Atl building could be shown. (See Atlpic.ppt)

The video rectangle shows a map of North America, featuring highlighted areas of the 8 centers. These are: (DIGITAL PICTURES OF THESE CENTERS TO BE INCLUDED HERE – note: Atlanta has two locations so it must be shown on map)

Toronto, Ontario, Montreal, Quebec, Boise, Idaho, Roseville, California, Mtn. View California, Loveland, Colorado, and Atlanta Georgia.

This map animates toward the ABC location. This image dissolves to a montage of ABC employees, and shots of the facilities.

Imagery of this section includes shots of the Call Center operations areas, the Briefing Center, computer facilities and individual workers and their screens.

This section aims to capture a techie look and feel of the ABC, while showing the human side via the faces and expressions of the employees. Diversity and

MUSIC HERE IS ONCE AGAIN ENERGETIC. THE NARRATION AND MUSIC ALLOW THE IMAGERY TO "BREATHE" AND DOMINATE WHEN APPROPRIATE.

NARRATOR

IN NORTH AMERICA, HP'S

E-DELIVERY ORGANIZATION

PROVIDES SUPPORT FROM EIGHT

STRATEGIC LOCATIONS THAT

INCLUDE OVER 2600 PROFESSIONALS

WITH AN INDUSTRY AVERAGE OF

OVER 18 YEARS OF EXPERIENCE.

ONE OF THESE LOCATIONS IS THE

ATLANTA BUSINESS CENTER. HERE,

HP PROFESSIONALS DRAW UPON

THEIR TECHNICAL EXPERTISE,

YEARS OF EXPERIENCE, COMMITMENT

TO CUSTOMER SATISFACTION AND

LOYALTY TO DELIVER WORLD-CLASS

SUPPORT.

experience are the guides
here.

A visual device places
certain employees and
employee groups in the frame
in a way to accentuate the
narrator's points. These
employees are chosen for
their appearance and
diversity.

EXPERIENCE MONTAGE

A series of shots feature
individuals and groups –
while a corresponding text
blurbs identifies them and
their corresponding years of
service.

For example: The shot is of
Frank Johnson. It freezes,
and the text super reveals –
"Frank Johnson, 25 years
experience"

Or the shot is that of the
"Printer Services Group, 136
years of experience"

This technique repeats 3-5
times.

Note: details are being
worked out and arrangements
being made for shoot and
stats.

WORKING AS INDIVIDUALS AND AS
PART OF A TEAM, HP ENGINEERS
ARE EMPOWERED TO GO THE EXTRA
MILE FOR THE CUSTOMER. OUR
PROFESSIONALS HAVE THE SPEED TO
ANSWER, THE POWER TO SOLVE AND
THE PASSION TO DO GREAT WORK.
AND EXPERIENCE?

MUSIC CHANGES FOR THE
EXPERIENCE MONTAGE.
PERCUSSION DOMINATES.

PROCESS AND FACILITIES

Imagery includes shots of
technology, computer
screens, professionals doing
their jobs.

Note: Show shots of Barrett

(barrett.ppt)

Camera shots of:

Screens of WMF, event
notification, and snapshot
of HAO.

NARRATOR

COMPLIMENTING THE ATLANTA

BUSINESS CENTER IS THE BARRETT

PARKWAY FACILITY, WHICH

PROVIDES ADDITIONAL HARDWARE,

SOFTWARE AND NETWORKING

RESOURCES FOR OUR CUSTOMERS. IN

BOTH CENTERS IN ATLANTA, HP

UTILIZES STATE OF THE ART TOOLS

AND METHODOLOGIES DESIGNED TO

MAXIMIZE EFFICIENCY, AND

PROVIDE LIGHTNING RESPONSE TO

CUSTOMERS. OUR BEST IN CLASS

PRACTICES INCLUDE A WORK FLOW

MANAGEMENT SYSTEM, EVENT

NOTIFICATION AND PROACTIVE

TOOLS.

ARMED WITH THESE TOOLS, OUR

PROFESSIONALS ARE READY WITH

SOLUTIONS FOR YOUR ALWAYS-ON

BUSINESS.

RECAP

Video is a montage of
activity throughout the ABC.
These are people engaged in
helping the customer.

NARRATOR

HP SERVICES CONTINUES to be YOUR
TRUSTED ADVISOR TO HELP YOU
TRANSFORM YOUR BUSINESS, DERIVE
MEASURABLE BUSINESS VALUE FROM

People at terminals, on
phones, drawing on
whiteboards, servicing
servers.

End on smiling employee.

FADE OUT.

YOUR IT INVESTMENTS, AND DELIVER
ONGOING CUSTOMER LOYALTY THROUGH
A BROAD IT SERVICES PORTFOLIO FOR
EVERY FACET OF YOUR CHANGING
BUSINESS NEEDS. AT HP, OUR
SERVICE PROFESSIONALS PROVIDE THE
SERVICES AND SUPPORT YOU NEED TO
KEEP YOUR ENVIRONMENT UP AND
RUNNING. OUR EXPERIENCED PEOPLE
EMPLOY PROVEN METHODOLOGIES TO
PROVIDE THE SPEED, POWER AND
PASSION TO MEET ANY CHALLENGE,
SOLVE AND SATISFY EVERY CUSTOMER.
WE'RE HERE FOR YOU.

Chapter 16: Unisys Briefing Center
Haven't we been here before?

The Executive Briefing Center pitch business continued to roll on for VisionFactory with a project for Unisys. Unisys was a huge company that helped other huge companies to streamline operations through technology, business services, consulting and who knows what else. The word e-Business comes to mind. This was a time that anything with an e in front of it was important. As I write this I realize that I never really knew what it was that Unisys did. I just know that we had a new client wanting a sexy new EBC, and armed with bullet points and a great 3D animator, we set out to make a video to pitch our vision of what it should be.

The information and script in this chapter provides another example of how client provided marketing points can be worked into a video presentation – in this case a walkthrough of the virtual space.

I.   Intro

- Conversational Dialogue
- Setup rationale for EBC
- Link in UNISYS need to express USP –
- Clever messaging – segues into walkthrough

II.   Scene A – Home Office

- Non-defined visitor in office type surrounding
- Discuss Pre-visit web

III.   Scene B – Reception

- Entering lobby – special touches
- Digital signage – projected waterfall screen (Need to POC)
- Visitors receive badge/ swipe card (and/or e-squirt)

IV.   Messaging Segue #1

- Why is corporate culture important to showcase?
- People make the difference
- Set anticipation for the visit

V.   Scene C – EBC entryway

- Kiosks for the web/email access within a personal "web wrapper" (use card for login
- Plasma "art" on wall springs to life and then present high-level UNISYS messages "du jour"

VI.   Messaging segue – Conference rooms

- "Look, you spend most of your day in a conference room. So how do you get the most out of it?"
- Collaborations, information, sharing
- Comfortable, accessible, user-friendly

VII.   Scene D – Meeting space

- Focus on Video conferencing
- Presentation - enhancements to power point
- Integrated room control and presentation (show total space access via custom WIN CE web application (HP Jornada?)

VIII.   Scene E - Dining

- Comfortable dining
- Ambient music available
- News Bar in corner (CNN FN feeds)

IX.   Messaging Segue #3

- Show the heart of UNISYS – the total solutions
- Up-sell clients by exposure to other, related solutions
- Purposeful WOW.

X.   Scene F – Center of Excellence

- Mixture of conf space, presentation space
- 3 v-mail kiosk stations in space
- projection of ?
- Working lab to support the demos
- Presenter can send digital collateral to personal website (sales function)
- E-squirt

XI.   Wrap Up

- EBC becomes the Heart of UNISYS
- Increase traffic and visibility
- Show it better, Track it better, sell it better

UNISYS EXECUTIVE BRIEFING CENTER

A Note about style:

The approach to this video involves dueling narrators. First there is a male voice that poses conceptual questions about the nature of a corporation's briefing program and what makes that program successful. The second voice is a female who answers these questions and concerns with the solution that VisionFactory is proposing.

The First voice is always accompanied by a composited montage of still imagery and animated text. The still imagery is conceptual in nature, relating to the spoken message. The text both encapsulates the message as well as hints at the unspoken answers. For example, the question "What entices business executives to commit to a solutions provider?" is accompanied with the literal text of the question as well as floating text of some answers – "Quality, service, value, image, brand…". Accompanying imagery may include people working in e-business environments, busy centers of commerce, abstract and metaphorical textures and photos. These segments form the intellectual framework for the more descriptive pieces of the presentation – the walkthroughs.

The second voice is that of answers. It is the voice that leads the viewer from thinking about to understanding how to create the most successful UNISYS Executive Briefing Center possible. This voice is the narrator of the visitor's journey through the EBC. 3D animation of the EBC experience is what accompanies this voice.

SCENE 1 – INTRODUCTION – Aftereffects animation - Text and stills

Music pipes up as a row of small images appear, scrolling horizontally in the lower third of the screen. Floating text joins the frame as the narrator speaks.

> NARRATOR 1:
> What entices business executives to commit to a solutions provider? Is it how they perceive your industry, your products, your value? How they perceive your company?

> NARRATOR 2:
> VisionFactory spent time thinking about UNISYS; exploring messages about your people , your brand and your value to the customer. Then we envisioned a space where those customers, current and future, are immersed in the UNISYS message – what it means to be the world's premiere e-Business solutions provider. Welcome to the UNISYS Executive briefing center.

TITLE FORMS AGAINST BLACK:

"UNISYS EXECUTIVE BRIEFING CENTER"

Fade to black

SCENE 2 – Pre-visit website

Fade up:

White title –"Before Visiting"

INT. CONFERENCE ROOM

Seated at the side of a table, just before a flat panel monitor is a young business woman. The camera pushes toward here, arcing to the screen as we get closer. Onscreen is a UNISYS website with details about a briefing center visit.

> NARRATOR 2 :
> The UNISYS Briefing Center experience begins long before the actual visit. Through a personalized pre-visit web presence, UNISYS sales staff can prepare guests for their visit and elicit customer feedback in planning the agenda and selecting UNISYS presentations. This first line of contact is the foundation for customized treatment of every EBC visitor.

The camera reaches the monitor screen as the images fades out.

SCENE 3 - RECEPTION

The camera passes through the front doors of the EBC. It moves toward the receptionist's desk which features a striking media sculpture involving a waterfall and projected imagery. The space is bright and features a wall treatment made from natural wood colored elements that form a wavelike surface.

The Camera moves toward the receptionist.

> NARRATOR 2:
> Arriving at the EBC, UNISYS guests are greeted by the reception staff and given a personalized smart card to use throughout the day. This card acts as a security badge as well as a interactive key for many customized touch points throughout the center. These points include areas of corporate messaging as well as customer and product specific information and few experiences that are just plain fun. In addition, the personalized card continues the one-to-one experience between the EBC staff and the visitors. This helps to ensure every guest's needs are met and every lead is fully explored.

CU on a UNISYS EBC smart card. The card is floating in space. It spins into a fixed position before the camera, just to the left side of the frame. As the narration unravels this frame adds three graphic circles that point to the card (features). These are:

- Security Badge
- Custom Media Key
- Access to Personal web space

FADE TO BLACK

SCENE 4 – CORPORATE CULTURE MESSAGING – Aftereffects Animation

The flow of images and words again occur against a black background. Words include "Image, Corporate DNA, Culture, Values, Confidence, Security, Innovation."

> NARRATOR 1:
> Why is corporate culture so important to showcase? Does a company's appearance really impact the bottom line? How can you convey your company's attitude and values?

Imagery becomes that of workers, happy and diverse, smiling and hip.

NARRATOR 2:
At UNISYS it's the people that make the difference. Unisys
people have the creativity, technical excellence, tenacity, and
can-do spirit to help their clients solve business problems.

DISSOLVE TO:

SCENE 5 – EBC ENTRYWAY

The camera moves from the lobby into the "inner lobby". This move is slow enough to take
in the cultural DNA pervasive in the design.

NARRATOR 2: (cont.)
The UNISYS EBC reflects the attitudes and the culture of these
people by providing a creative, exciting environment for the
staff and visitors. The entry to the EBC is such a space. Here
visitors receive a high level overview of the UNISYS story via
a unique media presentation. This space, designed to be both
striking and functional, becomes home base for the visitors.
The casual seating and web terminals provide visitors access
to their personal web space as well as other UNISYS
messaging. This space also introduces the power of the EBC's
many presentation tools. Here, the group leader can launch
different presentations and control lighting and sound using
his wireless device.

As the camera moves through the room, the artwork on the integrated wall plasma screens
transitions into the UNISYS overview video (FROM CD).

In close up the camera moves around to the screen of a PDA that is suspended in mid-air. On
the screen is a simple control system that includes a location button (currently it reads
"HOMEBASE"), a two slider controls for LIGHTING, and a Slider for SOUND. In
addition, in the center of the screen there are several icons that represent the high level media
most often presented in that room.

SPLITSCREEN - THE CLOSE UP OF THE PDA recedes into the left third of the screen as
the right two thirds becomes a wide shot of the room.

IN this split screen state we see the GUI of the PDA animate as if it is being manipulated,
and in the right frame we see the room response to these manipulations. (IN THE ROOM
VIEW THE SCREENS NOW SHOW A STATIC UNISYS LOGO). First the sound slider is
animated up, then light sliders are brought down – the room shot reacts in time. Then a
presentation icon is illuminated as if it is being launched. A status line reads "PLAYING".
(Need to sketch this interface). In the room view, the screens launch a different presentation.

FADE TO BLACK.

SCENE 6 – MESSAGING SEGUE – Conference Rooms

Title fades up – "MEETINGS"

Imagery is that of roll up your sleeves business men and women getting down to a good ole meeting.

>   NARRATOR 1:
>   Look we all know the drill, you spend the whole day in a
>   conference room, right? Isn't that where the real business is
>   done? Face to face, some overheads, legal pads. Bad coffee.
>
>   NARRATOR 2:
>   Meeting space is important, but it doesn't have to be dull.
>   Let's face it, 4 hours of Power Point can numb anyone's
>   senses.

SCENE 7 INT. MEETING SPACE

The camera glides into a the large conference room. Several workers are scatter throughout the room. It is very spacious, and modern looking. At the front corner of the room, by the rear projection screen stands a UNISYS saleswoman. See has before her a unique looking iNav presentation menu.

CLOSE UP on the media system (iNav menu)

ANGLE ON PROJECTION SCREEN
Video Conferencing layout with a remote person is onscreen.

Onscreen an animated product demo replaces the video conferencing.

>   NARRATOR 2: (cont.)
>   The UNISYS EBC meeting space is designed to be
>   comfortable, accessible, and user-friendly, while projecting a
>   modern, exciting image of the company's culture. Here
>   technology is used as an enhancement to the critical purpose of
>   face to face communication. We empower the UNISYS staff
>   with dynamic presentation support to inform and entertain their
>   guests with a variety of media as well as robust video

conferencing and product demo tie-ins. Equally important, the
backend system for media support allows simple uploading,
and retrieval for the EBC staff. This ensures that every group
receives a dynamic message based on their company's needs.

FADE TO BLACK.

SCENE 8 – DINING

TITLE FADES IN – "EBC DINING"
Camera shows a panorama of the dining space. It slowly glides through the space and the
people scatter around it. There is a news bar area playing CNN FN footage, as well as a
stock ticker above it.

> NARRATOR 2:
> During their productive business day, guests relax in the EBC
> dining facility to enjoy a casual lunch. The dining area features
> ambient music and a media bar where current financial feeds
> keep visitors informed during their break.

SCENE 9 – MESSAGING SEGUE – Center of Excellence

NARRATOR 1:
What about products and solutions? I want to see the HEART of UNISYS? How can I see
the breadth of what they have to offer and see it in action?

SCENE 10 – CENTER OF EXCELLENCE

Camera moves slowly to reveal the technology arcade that is the Center of Excellence.

> NARRATOR 2:
> The featured attraction of the UNISYS EBC is the Center of
> Excellence. Here guests are immersed in UNISYS solutions in
> a theatrical environment that exploits technology and design to
> showcase value. The thematic boldness of the Center of
> Excellence sets UNISYS apart from traditional solutions
> providers. As a mixture of conference space, demonstration
> areas and a working lab, the Center of Excellence always
> features exciting UNISYS solutions. Here the presenter has a
> dramatic canvas to deliver product, line of business and
> corporate messaging. Wireless connectivity to media and
> demonstrations empowers the presenter with a healthy mixture
> of substance and showbiz to both wow and enlighten the

visitors. With tie-ins to the personal webspace function of the center, The COE presents visitors many ways to bookmark and send key marketing points to their colleagues. In addition, video mail kiosks provide an entertaining way to say hi from UNISYS.

FADE TO BLACK.

SCENE 11 – WRAP UP

Text and imagery reflecting the narration.

> NARRATOR 1:
> So, for corporate image, product and solution messaging, face to face interaction, and a vision of the value of UNISYS, you're saying there's one place that brings it all together?

Montage area animations throughout the video.

> NARRATOR 2:
> One place. A place to showcase the vision and culture of the world's leading e-Business solutions provider. A place the builds on the culture of creativity, service, quality and value. The UNISYS Executive Briefing Center.

END ON UNISYS LOGO

FADE OUT.

NOTES:
WRAP UP
FOR ENDING?

In more than 100 countries around the world, leading financial services institutions, airlines, communications providers, commercial market leaders, and government agencies rely on Unisys. We help them apply information technology to streamline operations ... anticipate and adapt to change ... attract and retain new clients ... enable executives to make informed decisions ... support front-line employees responding to customer needs ... and achieve new levels of competitiveness and success.

In the early 2000's one of VisionFactory's clients found themselves in a rapid period of growth. Raytheon was being called upon to supply a large amount of missiles and other high tech weapons for the war efforts in Afghanistan and eventually Iraq. The national mood was belligerent and many weapons manufacturers were riding that attitude to the bank. Raytheon was also expanding into network connected military areas, pioneering new products and systems that married the IP network with battlefield strategy. To help convey some of these new concepts and to make more accessible their entire product line, Raytheon turned to VisionFacotry to help create interactive media for tradeshow and briefing center displays.

One project from Raytheon was for a new briefing center which featured networking demonstrations, a larger theater space and a working lab space. They needed to create an overview video about the space to be used as a welcome piece for visiting dignitaries. The Netcentric Integration and Experimentation Center project would be a combination of live action footage shot within the new space and 3D renderings of different ways the space could be used. Since the video would be presented on the large screen in the center's theater, we knew we wanted a high quality piece that looked and sounded great, so the production was shot on HD and we created a Dolby surround soundtrack for the piece. For the live action footage, my friend Matt Hedt and I travelled to the location with a jib and doorway dolly to capture the interior shots. Shooting in HD and renting a wide angle lens helped to capture some shots that seamlessly worked alongside the 3D renderings of the space. At times it was difficult to tell which was which.

Included here is the working script for the project. You'll notice some changes are preserved as they happened.

Raytheon Netcentric Integration and Experimentation Center - Tidewater
Intro Script
6/15/2006 v2

1. Introduction

Music Mixes up. It is warm and inviting.

Exterior of the Tidewater Facility with Raytheon signage dissolves to gliding shot though the center's lobby, following two people as they make their way toward the reception area. Other shots here may include Raytheon Displays in the lobby, etc., all with flowing camera moves.

> NARRATOR
> Welcome to the Raytheon Netcentric Integration and Experimentation Center – Tidewater; a collaborative, virtual environment bringing together Raytheon centers of excellence from around the globe, to ~~design state-of-the-art net-enabled architectures and applications~~ provide our customers a portal into the company's vast engineering resources.

Midway, live video dissolves into a composite screen of collaboration and simulation video, animations, and demonstration imagery as the music becomes much more techie and energetic.

Possible title here at bottom of the screen "**Netcentric Integration and Experimentation Center - Tidewater**" transitions to the letters **NIEC-T**.

2. Viz 3D Room

An overhead 3D extrusion of the Center floor plan glides toward the more detailed area of the Viz Center. The lighting grid, speakers and projection screen are highlighted as the narration plays out. The 3D image dissolves to video of a presentation within the room as audience members watch.

> EFX: low rumble starts; atmospheric sound ambience

> NARRATOR
> In the Visualization Center you witness a full spectrum of capabilities for high fidelity ~~distributed modeling and simulation~~ demonstration of Raytheon technologies and Mission System Integration capacity.

Narrator speaks first and then we hear sound build out of each speaker location.

> NARRATOR
> Sound envelops you, creating a dramatic sense of immersion.

> EFX: 5.1 channel audio focuses sound out of each speaker location on cue (jets fly back to front, missiles fly left to right, communication chatter from front)

Animation adds speaker locations with emanating waves (in sync with the directed sound)

NARRATOR
Theatrical lighting establishes the visitor's operating environment.

EFX: bright, ethereal sound backdrop

Animation layers in the theatrical lighting grid; lights begin the glow on the grid

NARRATOR
The Visualization Center's video wall delivers over 6 mega-pixels of high fidelity imaging in support of our multi-site distributed simulations.

EFX: Full 5.1 sound effects supporting the main video wall imagery; isolate various sound files associated with some of the tiled animations These images don't have to be only DoD elements.

Animation 3D camera zooms toward video wall to cover it full screen

NARRATOR
Working in unison, all audio-visual capabilities contribute to an immersive experience.

3. The Lab

The Overhead 3D model returns, now moving toward the Lab. The camera glides toward a simulation area made up of three video displays as the 3D image dissolves to a booming video shot of two people and an operator examining the demonstration.

NARRATOR
In the Lab you will experience the latest Netcentric applications in action, as we harness the power of live, multi-site distributive simulations and experimentation.

4. Customer Success

A series of elegantly moving shots of different areas of the NIEC including the conference rooms and other interaction points. Shots should include Raytheon theming, demonstrations, displays etc. When available, show people interacting.

NARRATOR
At Raytheon, customer success is our mission. To this end, the Network Netcentric Integration Experimentation Center creates an environment of comfort and collaboration with over 6000 8000 square feet of conference and conference room and exhibit space.
[I can use the lab for exhibit space...so over 3000 sf of conference and 5000 lab/exhibit space]

5. Conclusion

EFX: Music in - spirited, strong

Animation 3D camera zooms back out to reveal the entire space; camera continues to creep away, making the space begin to disappear into the distance.

NARRATOR
Welcome to the future of netcentric operations. (*slight beat*)
The Raytheon Netcentric Integration and Experimentation Center -
Tidewater.

SLOW DISSOLVE to NIEC title

EFX: music crescendo

EFX: low rumble/atmospheric sound

CROSS DISSOLVE to Raytheon Logo Should be GIANT to cover as much of the wall as possible

EFX: music/sounds out

Hold on logo – END

Scriptwriting is generally thought of as a linear thing. Sure, ideas come in different order and the job of the writer is to arrange them into a nice flow that makes sense and holds the viewer, but in general the thinking is a beginning, middle and end that flow nicely in chronological order. Writing a narrative is like creating a small slice of life, usually in the same order that it might happen.

Writing for an interactive presentation is a completely different thing. It is like designing a game or a "build your own adventure" story. There is still a structure, but it is the branching based on user choices that make things more complex. It's also a fun process, forcing you to think of multiple possibilities and to find ways to bring the user back to a common area. I write "user" here instead of "viewer" because an interactive project involves the audience. It requires regular points of decision and action on their part. The flow of the story or game or learning activity can vary greatly based on the user's actions. They control the flow.

Writing an interactive piece poses a few new challenges over writing a traditional script. The main challenge is creating a flow chart that identifies all of the possible routes that the story will take. There is a game-like logic to creating this structure, and when done well, it can be very rewarding. Choosing ways to present choices to the user and where these choices will lead is an exercise in becoming the audience. You must imagine what you can get away with. You must ask questions like "Is the clever?" or "Is this annoying". Then you have to settle on an outline of the content areas and interactive triggers, and then start filling in the boxes.

An interactive writer must be versatile, understanding the content of the subject matter and having a grasp of how the piece will be created. Understanding the programming involved in creating an interactive piece can be as important as getting the topic right. The main reason for this is that the script must reach three audiences – the client who must get a sense of the final product long before it is created, the programmer who must connect the dots to make a user friendly and entertaining product, and the user who will ultimately be putting the creation through its paces. As the writer, you must work with all three audiences in mind, dancing your way between story and the more complex programming notes involved. Sometimes referencing common elements like a video game can help bridge the gap between the two. Other times simply writing up the experience will help those dependent on the script to understand your vision. Flow charts and visual mockups are also essential.

Software development tools vary greatly, but all accept user input in a few basic ways. Writing for a DVD for instance limits the user interactivity to a few menu choices from a remote control. This opens up opportunities to write branching points of interactivity, but not so much real-time user interaction. Writing for a PC or MAC application opens interactivity up to keystrokes, mouse movements, mouse clicks and much more behind the scenes interactivity based on user input and information. With the development of Android and iOS devices like smart phones, and tablets devices, the accelerometer has been added to the mix, allowing for tilting and movements of the device itself as a user input. Clearly all of these interactions provide the programmer and script writer a variety of ways to build a story where the user becomes an integral part of how things play out. This landscape opens up the creative toolbox for the writer, enabling more and more immersive interactive projects.

For one of our Nortel projects we had to create a series of teaching tools for an interactive area called SimSpace. These simulations would act as both an educational exercise and a demonstration of different networking products. For one such project I wrote a script for a telephony product called Centrex. The game-like nature of the demonstration is best illustrated by the flow chart which also provides the framework for the individual script elements. Having a great deal of experience since I first wrote this interactive script, I can see a number of ways that I would now make it more visual. The complexity of creating all of the elements required for a branching story requires a special approach to organizing the script. So with that apology addressed, enjoy the Centrex Simulation.

Centrex Unlimited SimSpace Simulation

Scriptwriter: Steve White

This script was the foundation for an interactive product experience simulation at Nortel Networks Executive Briefing Center in RTP, NC. The interactive station was used to introduce the Centrex Unlimited product line in an entertaining, game-like environment.

The script incorporates role playing, and decision based branching that allows the user to explore first person, real world simulations, while presenting a concurrent 40,000 foot view of the network operations that enable the product line.

The simulation was produced in August, 1999.

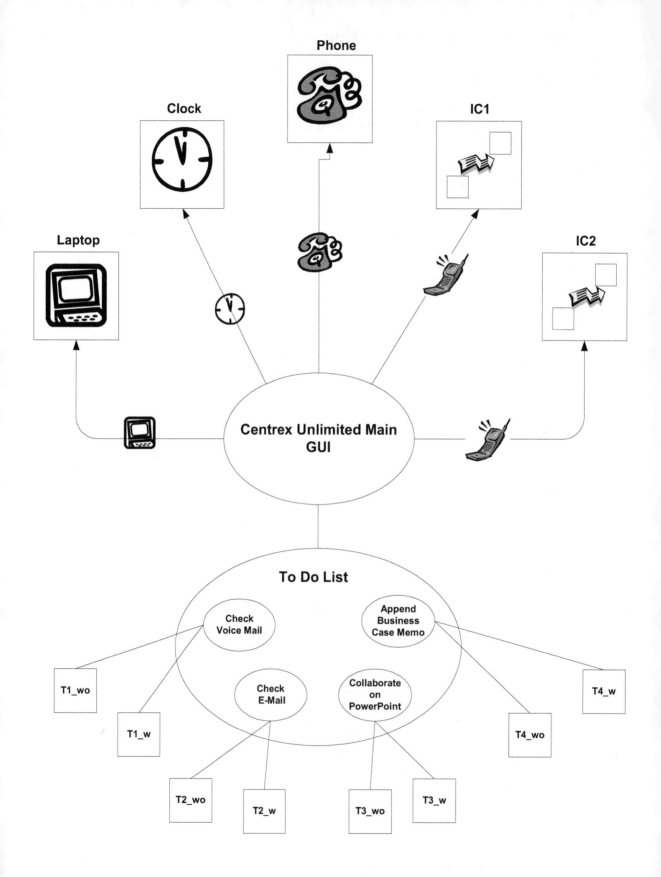

Destination Nortel Networks
Centrex Unlimited
Simulation

Road Warrior

The Set-Up
The user plays the role of a Road Warrior. This Road Warrior, on a layover in an airline's Executive Club, learns that his or her connecting flight has been changed. The Road Warrior now has 25 minutes rather than an hour to accomplish the tasks on his or her to-do list. The tools available include a laptop, a telephone and a Centrex Unlimited button. They can use any combination of those tools to get their tasks done in time. The time is tracked by a "ticking clock" that rolls off the task minutes based on each choice.

The To-Do List
- Check Voice Mail
- Check E-mail
- Collaborate on a PowerPoint document
- Make changes to a business case document (uses CVA to place call)
- *Receive an incoming call (shows twinning when call is placed and wireless portion of the network)

The Rules
Working against a countdown, the user identifies the task they want to accomplish. He or she then chooses whether they want to use the telephone or the laptop with Centrex Unlimited power. Using the telephone immediately subtracts time from the countdown clock. In the telephone world, each task is worth 7 minutes. So, if a user were to choose to accomplish all the tasks with the telephone, they would miss their flight. The user can toggle between the telephone and Centrex Unlimited application to accomplish a task; however, once they've chosen the telephone option, they've lost those minutes.

If a user chooses Centrex Unlimited, they accomplish all tasks with time to spare. Accomplishing each task using Centrex Unlimited deducts only 2 minutes from the countdown clock.

The Scenarios

Check voice mail
Without Centrex Unlimited – Using the telephone, the user dials many numbers to connect to their voice mailbox. User loses 7 minutes; page of jumbled notes appears on the screen; user leaves 5 messages and must return two completed calls with additional information; cannot move to other tasks until all messages are heard.

With Centrex Unlimited – User's GUI presents all the user's messages; they see results each time they click on a message; a "unified messaging" application allows the user to check all messages, accomplishing all three message review tasks. To illustrate the flexibility of unified messaging, the user can "skip" extraneous messages and attend to those that relate to the tasks at hand. 2 minutes

Check E-mail
Without Centrex Unlimited – User connects to their account using the laptop. They click to respond to each message. They lose 7 minutes for this individual task.

With Centrex Unlimited – User's GUI presents all the user's messages; they see results each time they click on a message; a "unified messaging" application allows the user to check all messages, accomplishing all three message review tasks.

Collaborate on a PowerPoint document
Without Centrex Unlimited – Using the telephone and the laptop, a user calls their colleague and refers to the PowerPoint document on their screen; the colleague agrees to make the discussed changes and e-mail the results; user loses 7 minutes.

With Centrex Unlimited – The user is able to talk to a colleague while sharing the same computer screen. Collaborating, the two users edit the document in real time. Three minutes

Make changes to a business case document
Without Centrex Unlimited – The user calls a colleague to discuss a document. He tries to make changes over the phone while fumbling with the laptop. The conversation here is confused including words like "Wait a minute, what version are you looking at? No, that's from last week." Ten minutes

With Centrex Unlimited – The user is able to talk to his colleague while they both edit the document. "This looks great! I'm glad we're on the same page."
Three minutes

Receive call
Without Centrex Unlimited – The end user watches a network as his or her office phone rings and is ultimately sent to voice mail. Flash forward to the Road Warrior checking messages when they arrive in the next city.   The message on voice mail is, "No need to continue your trip. The customer agreement has been signed. Come on home."

With Centrex Unlimited – The incoming call is a bonus for using Centrex Unlimited to accomplish the tasks. When the call originates, the network view shows the twinning of the user's office and the cell phone. The user answers the cell phone and the message is, "No need to continue your trip. The customer agreement has been signed. Come on home."

The Interface
The majority of the simulation will take place at the "Virtual Road Warrior Office" at the airport Admiral's Club. The User will be represented by a silhouette seated before a laptop computer and telephone set. He will also use a Star Set with the laptop when using Centrex Unlimited features.

At times video pop-up characters will egg the user in one direction or another. For instance a leisure-suit clad yokel will say, "Just use the old phone. It's reliable. It always works. Features Shmeatures." And a sharp dressed professional will chime in, "Centrex Unlimited gives you all the Centrex features you expect at the office and much more anytime, anywhere." These characters will aid in contrasting the old and new way as well as provide another way to deliver the marketing points for Centrex Unlimited.

To show the network path and elements, a network view will be presented when necessary. For instance, when the incoming call is placed, the network view will show the twinning feature as well as the wireless portion of the network. This network view will also allow information of each Centrex Unlimited component to be explored with the click of a mouse.

Video and audio elements will also be used when appropriate to represent the edge of the network during the network view.

The Script

Introduction:
SOUND of a landing plane covers the voice over. The plane taxis as the VO plays out. Against a Black screen the outline of the word "**Centrex**" begins to form to the left side of the screen, with the directional flow of clouds just behind it. It is as if the outline of the font is a window to a moving sky. This is a really slow reveal.

> NARRATOR:
> Today's Road Warriors face many communications challenges everyday. Every second counts when your business is on the line.

The Word "**Unlimited**" begins to form beside the Word Centrex. Also a slow reveal, as the background image becomes much brighter until finally turning white leaving the title "**Centrex Unlimited**".

> NARRATOR: (cont.)
> At the office, the powerful features of Centrex have made business communications more efficient. Now Centrex Unlimited brings the power of Centrex to the entire communications network. Centrex Unlimited, Any Service, Anywhere, Anytime.

The audio background picks up with a stewardess' voice.

> STEWARDESS:
> Weather today is a sunny 65 degrees. We hope you enjoy your stay in Springfield or wherever your destination may be.

The title fades to Black

The Airline's Executive club desk area fades up to a somewhat muted state.

TEXT reveals to Identify the location accompanied by a subtle sound effect:

Jaco International Airport
Executive Lounge
3:35 PM

The scene fully fades in to a close-up of the desk area over the shoulder of the silhouetted character. On the desk appears an open laptop with a Star headset attached, a cell phone, and the phone set that is already there. Also there is an open notepad. On the wall is a round clock. It is 3:35. A full glass of tea with a little umbrella in it resides in the upper right hand corner of the desk.

Clicking on the notepad presents the "Things to do" list. Scribbled neatly are the following items:
- **Check Voice Mail**
- **Check E-mail**
- **Call Janet about Presentation**
- **Make changes to business case document**
- **Check Pricing on XJ7 Component**

Clicking on individual items on the notepad launches that item's sequence.
Clicking on a small frayed corner of the notepad turns the page to a scribble of a beach in the Bahamas. The scene features a smiling stickman-our character, with the word scribbled under it – "me". Clicking on this page turns it back to the list. Clicking outside of the list returns to the wider view of the desk.

Clicking on the laptop brings the **screen forward full-screen**. It shows the current state of the laptop- at first that state is a Windows' desktop for Conglomo Enterprises. It **shows common icons above a Conglomo logo**.
These include:
- **Power Point Icon for "Presentation"**
- **Word Doc. Icon for "Business Case"**
- **A video icon for "Centrex Unlimited"** (clicking this plays a brief Centrex Unlimited Video Clip like in the Hub)
- **Unified Messaging (or Check Messages) Icon**

Clicking on the **clock** brings it full-screen and it ticks annoyingly. Clicking it again reverses the action.

Clicking the **phone** set takes it off the hook and gives a dialtone.

Clicking on the **glass** and there is sound of gulping, and the tea level goes down slightly. This is followed by an "Ahhhhhhh." This can be done 5 times until the glass is empty.

IC1 – Incoming call 1 (answer by clicking on Cell phone)
This is the call from the secretary that sets up the situation.

Scene: IC1
After a moment the cell phone rings. Clicking on the brings it to the foreground. This image begins collapsing into a small corner of a network diagram. This diagram shows the location of the airport (with the window of our character), as well as the internal structure of a common phone network. **See diagram – Without Centrex Unlimited**

At one end of the Network is a representation of an office building. A secretary begins talking as a pop up **image of her** appears over the existing Centrex Site in the upper left side. The network shows the path of the call. It goes from the secretary through the PTSN to a DMS-100 wireless port to a tower and over the air to the airport. This establishes the network view, which we will use more often as we show the Centrex and non-Centrex way.

> SECRETARY:
> Good news boss, I was able to push up your connecting flight.
> Be at Gate 12 by four o'clock and you're all set. I guess
> you've got about 25 minutes to get that work done. See you
> when you get back.

Staying on the Network view.

> NARRATOR:
> With traditional wireless service, one number is required
> for a wireless phone and another is required for the office.

555-6028 appears over the airport location the wireless phone image beside it
555-1234 appears over the Branch office area

> NARRATOR: (cont.)
> With Nortel Networks' Integrated Wireless component of Centrex Unlimited,
local number portability and twinning features allow for more efficient mobility and single voicemail services. Integrated Wireless also extends the feature rich DMSS-100 Centrex services to the road warrior, creating a powerful portable office.

The Network Illuminates connections via "packets" during the Twinning, Voice Mail language.

The view changes back to our character at the desk. The clock shows 3:35. Ticking sound is evident, though it fades slowly after 10 seconds.

To-Do List Scenes

The Simulation plays out a total of 10 scenarios. These are the four tasks on the to do list shown both without Centrex Unlimited (or over standard PSTN) and with Centrex Unlimited.

Each scene is linear once the choice has been made. The scenario goes like this:

➢ Click on To-Do List
➢ Choose Item
➢ GUI Presents the options – Standard Phone Network, Centrex Unlimited
➢ Linear animation plays out showing user activity and network path. Narration explains what's happening.
➢ Animation ends- time "toll" is reported
➢ Choice is presented to see the same task the other way (no time penalty applies here)

The scene codes are as follows:

T1_wo
Task One – Check Voice mail without Centrex Unlimited

T1_w
Task One – Check Voice mail with Centrex Unlimited

T2_wo
Task Two - Check Email without Centrex Unlimited

T2_w
Task Two – Check Email with Centrex Unlimited

T3_wo
Task Three – Collaborate on Power Point Document Without Centrex Unlimited

T3_w
Task Three – Collaborate on Power Point Document with Centrex Unlimited

T4_wo
Task Four – Append Business Case Memo without Centrex Unlimited

T4_w
Task Four – Append Business Case Memo with Centrex Unlimited

T5_wo
Task Five – Check XJ7 Module Pricing over PSTN (shows hold time)

T5_w
Task Five – Check XJ7 Pricing over Internet Enabled Call Center

IC1 – Incoming call 1 (answer by clicking on Cell phone)
This is the call from the secretary that sets up the situation.

IC2 – Incoming call 2

This is the call at the end of the sequence that rewards you with a first class ticket. (Only if you've beat the clock)

IC3 – Incoming call 3
This call comes in if you've taken too much time. You've missed your plane and have an overnight layover.

Fleshed out scenes:

T1_wo
Task One – Check Voice mail without Centrex Unlimited

The PSTN View

At the bottom left side a small image a telephone handset appears in the Airport area of the network. The path of the call is shown in the network as a glowing red connection from the airport to the PSTN cloud to the DMS-100 at the edge of the PSTN connected to an office building using existing Centrex services.

(Does the VM reside on the DMS100? Or inside of the office building? Need to know this.) The Voice Mail system shows animated activity while the VM's are playing.

The sounds of Dialtone, Touch tones and Voice Mail play out.

You have 7 new messages. First Message:
Hello Mr. Robinson. My name is Jill Streets, and I want to offer you my financial planning services . . . . BEEP. (Bob cuts her off)

Second Message
Bob, this is Pete from North Shore Lobster Company. . . BEEP

Third Message
Bob, Jerry Stein. We need to hook up on that Business case document before you leave. Give me a call as soon as you get this message.

Narrator:
For the traditional Road Warrior, Voice Mail is a very linear thing. But sometimes the important messages are buried in the not so important ones.

The audio ends. Two buttons appear at the bottom of the screen.
- View example with Centrex Unlimited **(T1_w)**
- Return to Desktop **(DESKTOP)**

T1_w
Task One – Check Voice mail with Centrex Unlimited

The Laptop comes to the forefront. The **Unified messaging GUI** (to be created based on Outlook) shows an Outlook-like menu system that acts out connecting and checking messages. The menu shows the seven current messages in text form. (Use GUI's provided by Bill Barnhill).

The laptop screen collapses into the corner of the Centrex Unlimited Network Diagram, and the connection through the Managed IP network to the DMS 100 Switch is illuminated.

Narrator:
The IP connection allows the Road Warrior access to all of the powerful Centrex features he normally uses at the office, plus developing software allows unified voice and email messaging.

The Laptop screen explodes back to the forefront. Bob clicks on the one message from Jerry Stein. It plays.

Jerry Stein
Bob, Jerry Stein. We need to hook up on that Business case document before you leave. Give me a call as soon as you get this message.

Bob clicks the Return call button:
The phone Rings:

The Laptop screen collapses into the network diagram again. Another path (this one a different color) traces the new call from the airport, through the IP Network and to the Branch office at the bottom right corner. There pops up Jerry Stein in front of his computer.

Jerry Stein:
Conglomo, this is Jerry.

Bob
Jerry, I got your message. You going to be around the next few minutes?

Jerry
Yeah.

Bob
Great. I need to take care of a few things then we'll talk about the business case.

The audio ends. Two buttons appear at the bottom of the screen.
- View example without Centrex Unlimited **(T1_wo)**
- Return to Desktop **(DESKTOP)**

T2_wo
Task Two - Check Email without Centrex Unlimited

The Laptop comes to the foreground. Dial-up sequence starts, complete with modem cries. The first try is busy. The connection starts again and gets through. The "connection" window pops up.

The laptop screen collapses into the PSTN. The network path lights up connecting from airport, to PSTN cloud, to ISP to Internet cloud.

> Narrator
> The Public switched Telephone network wasn't made for data traffic. Modem limitations, busy signals, dedicated lines, and low bandwidth are just some of the problems inherent with data traffic over the existing network.

The Laptop screen explodes again.
The Outlook looking interface shows several new messages. One Reads:

"Bob, We really need to make these changes in Power Point. Get in touch with me soon. I'll be working at home this week. Thanks, Janet."

The laptop screen collapses again to the network view.

> Narrator
> The explosion of the Internet and killer apps like email have changed the communications landscape forever. With so many ways to get in touch, important information sometimes slips through the cracks, especially in today's chaotic work environment. This illuminates the need for a powerful, flexible unified messaging solution.

The audio ends. Two buttons appear at the bottom of the screen.
- View example with Centrex Unlimited **(T2_w)**
- Return to Desktop **(DESKTOP)**

T2_w
Task Two – Check Email with Centrex Unlimited

The laptop screen comes forward. The cursor moves to the Unified Messaging Icon and launches the Messaging screen.

The laptop screen collapses into the Centrex Unlimited network. The path lights up from the airport to the Managed IP network.

> Narrator:
> With an always on Packet-based connection, Centrex Unlimited enables access to email, voice mail and all the mature features of the DMS-100 Centrex services. The Road Warrior has a portable office that provides access to a variety of communication tools through Unified messaging.

Laptop explodes again.
The Outlook looking interface shows several new messages. The One that opens in a window reads:

"Bob, We really need to make these changes in Power Point. Get in touch with me soon. I'll be working at home this week. Thanks, Janet."

The laptop screen collapses again.

The audio ends. Two buttons appear at the bottom of the screen.
- View example without Centrex Unlimited **(T3_wo)**
- Return to Desktop **(DESKTOP)**

T3_wo
Task Three – Collaborate on PowerPoint Document without Centrex Unlimited

The laptop comes full screen. It shows the desktop view with a few icons. The cursor clicks on a PowerPoint doc that opens. The title screen reads "Conglomo Proposal: A Better Future through Plastics"

This view collapses in the corner of the PSTN View.

At the bottom left side, a small image of our character appears with the Airport area of the network.

The sounds of Dialtone, Touch tones play out.

The path of the call is shown in the network as a glowing red connection from the airport to the PSTN cloud to the DMS-100 at the edge of the PSTN connected to a telecommuter's home/ office.

An image of a woman on a phone in front of a computer appears in the upper right corner with the telecommuter section.

> Janet:
> Hello.

> Bob:
> Hi Janet. I got your email about the presentation. I've got it open in front of me. What do we need to change?

The window in Janet's side changes to a computer screen. Bob's does too.

> Janet:
> Can you go to slide 8?

Both screens flip through some slides. They stop, but are clearly different. Janet's slide has a series of bullets. Bob's is a picture of an Eskimo.

> Janet:
> OK. We need to change the third bullet to read: Greater insulation capacity.

> Bob:
> Third bullet? I don't have any bullets. Slide 8 is the Eskimo slide.

> Janet:
> The Eskimo slide. Wait a minute. What version do you have?

> Bob:
> Version 4.

Janet:
Oh. Look we're up to version 18 already. I think I'll have to email this to you. You can dial up from there, can't you?

The screen remains on the network with the two slides in their respective corners.

Narrator:
Collaboration on electronic documents can be a nightmare when you're on the road. The IP-based infrastructure of Centrex Unlimited will enable both Voice and data communication on the same line for the road, the office and telecommuters, making long distance collaboration a snap.

The audio ends. Two buttons appear at the bottom of the screen.
- View example with Centrex Unlimited **(T3_w)**
- Return to Desktop **(DESKTOP)**

T3_w
Task Three – Collaborate on PowerPoint Document With Centrex Unlimited

The laptop screen comes forward. The Unified Messaging screen is present.

The contact card for Janet Matheson comes up and the "call" button is clicked.

The laptop screen collapses into the Centrex Unlimited network. The path lights up from the airport to the Managed IP network to the upper right corner through a 1meg modem to the telecommuter's home/office.

Narrator:
The Centrex Unlimited infrastructure delivers simultaneous voice and data to the telecommuter through the use of the 1meg modem.

An image of a woman on a phone in front of a computer appears in the upper right hand corner with the telecommuter section.

Janet:
Hello.

Bob:
Hi Janet. I got your email about the PowerPoint. I've got it open in front of me. What do we need to change?

Both views switch to computer screens. Bob's view includes a star headset in the foreground. The PowerPoint slide title screen reads "Conglomo Proposal: A Better Future through Plastics"

Bob's cursor clicks on the "Share Document" button.

Janet:
Let's see.

Back to network view:
The window in Janet's side changes to a computer screen. Bob's does too.
Both screens flip through some slides. Past the title, past an Eskimo, to slide 8 which shows
some bullets.

> Janet:
> Slide 8. We're changing the 3rd bullet to read "Greater insulation capacity"

The screens change at the same time.

The screen remains on the network with the two slides in their respective corners. They
cycle through 4 other slides together.

> Narrator:
> Collaboration on electronic documents is crucial to smart business. The IP-
> based infrastructure of Centrex Unlimited enables both Voice and data
> communication on the same line on the road, at the office, and for
> telecommuters. And 3rd party software development will open up a world of
> customized communication solutions for file sharing, collaboration and more.

The audio ends. Two buttons appear at the bottom of the screen.
- View example without Centrex Unlimited **(T4_wo)**
- Return to Desktop **(DESKTOP)**

T4_wo
Task Four – Append Business Case Memo without Centrex Unlimited

The laptop comes full screen. It shows the desktop view with a few icons. The cursor clicks
on a Word document that opens. The title screen reads "Plastico – Plastic Company, Inc. A
Case for Change"

The screen cuts to:

The laptop screen and the telephone are seen over the shoulder of our Character. He has
the Headset to his ear. This view collapses in the corner of the PSTN View.

At the bottom left side a small image of our character appears with the Airport area of the
network.

The sounds of Dialtone, Touch tones play out.

The path of the call is shown in the network as a glowing red connection from the airport to
the PSTN cloud to the Branch Office at the lower right side.

An image of a woman on a phone appears in the lower right corner at the branch office.

> Secretary:
> Conglomo Enterprises. How may I direct your call?

Bob:
I need to speak with Jerry Stein.

Secretary:
One moment please.

The sound of being on hold. **Elevator music** kicks in.

Narrator:
Ever notice how you're put on hold precisely when you don't have time for it?

Secretary:
What was that name again?

Bob:
Jerry Stein

The sound of being on hold. Elevator music kicks in. Finally, the phone rings. The image in the corner changes to Jerry Stein in front of his computer with his telephone.

Jerry:
Jerry Stein.

Bob:
Hey Jerry. I'm running low on time. Can you quickly run me through those changes?

Jerry:
Sure. Actually I just had a copy faxed over to the desk at the Executive club. It's probably just as fast for you to type them in as it would be for me to try to tell you over the phone.

Bob:
Oh, they just brought it to me. It's a little smeared.

Back on the desktop view. The **crumpled fax** is on the desk with the other items.

Jerry:
Don't worry partner. I'm sure you'll figure it out.

Narrator:
When the bottom line is the success of your business and every second counts, you
don't need to take any chances. The powerful features of Centrex Unlimited provide business users with the valuable tools that take the uncertainty out of communicating.
The IP-based infrastructure of Centrex Unlimited will enable both voice and data communication on the same line for the road, the office and telecommuters.

The audio ends. Two buttons appear at the bottom of the screen.

- View example with Centrex Unlimited **(T4_w)**
- Return to Desktop **(DESKTOP)**

T4_w
Task Four – Append Business Case Memo with Centrex Unlimited

The laptop screen. The Unified Messaging screen is present. The Star headset is in the foreground.

Bob clicks the "Branch Office" icon to dial. The Icon looks like a small phone.

The laptop screen collapses into the Centrex Unlimited network. The path lights up from the airport to the Managed IP network to a DMS 100 the lower right to the branch office. A CVABD icon lights up in the network connection between the DMS-100 and the Branch Office.

> Narrator:
> Services like Centrex Voice Activated Business Directory or CVABD bring powerful call routing capabilities to a business.

CVABD Voice:
Welcome to Conglomo Corporation's Voice Attendant. Please state an employee name.

> Bob:
> Jerry Stein

> CVA Voice:
> Jerry Stein… (pause) Dialing.

Rings. The image in the corner changes to Jerry Stein in front of his computer with his telephone.

> Jerry:
> Jerry Stein

> Bob:
> Hey Jerry. I'm running low on time. Can you quickly run me through those changes?

> Jerry:
> Sure. I'll open it up in sharing mode.

Bob's Laptop comes to the forefront. He looks at the laptop and is wearing a Star Headset. On the laptop is the word document titled "Plastico – Plastic Company, Inc. A Case for Change"

In the document some text is highlighted, deleted and a new sentence is typed.

> Narrator:
> Collaboration on electronic documents is crucial to smart business. The IP-based infrastructure of Centrex Unlimited enables both voice and data

communication on the same line on the road, at the office and for telecommuters. And 3rd party software collaboration will open up a world of customized communication solutions for file sharing, collaboration and more.

This audio trails off as the view switches.

Back to network view:

The screens change simultaneously.

The screen remains on the network with the two slides in their respective corners. They cycle through 4 other slides together. The windows at the airport and branch now show the same document being scrolled and occasionally highlighted.

The audio ends. Two buttons appear at the bottom of the screen.
- View example without Centrex Unlimited **(T4_wo)**
- Return to Desktop **(DESKTOP)**

T5_wo
Task five – Check Pricing of XJ7 Module via Kaylee Enterprises website without Centrex Unilimted

Laptop comes to the forefront. Dialup sequence and open webpage for Kaylee Enterprises. www.kayleeint.com

Cursor highlights the phone number and then cursor presses disconnect button on laptop.

Meridian Handset comes into foreground. Sounds: **Dialtone, ring**

> RECORDING:
> Thanks for calling Kaylee Enterprises All of our customer service representatives are busy assisting other customers. Your expected hold time is 6 minutes.

Elevator music begins. Reminiscent of Gilbert O'Sullivan's "Alone Again Naturally"

> NARRATOR:
> Traditional call centers offer only one way to receive customer service inquiries. Heavy call traffic can lead to annoying hold times and lost opportunities.

The audio ends. Two buttons appear at the bottom of the screen.
- View example without Centrex Unlimited **(T5_w)**
Return to Desktop **(DESKTOP)**

T5_w
Task Five With Centrex Unlimited – Checking price of XJ7 Module from Kaylee Enterprises.com

Laptop Browser opens.
www.kayleeint.com
Page shows the XJ7 Module – a funky plastic device of unknown use. On the page is a button for the Sales Call Center.

It says click here for Internet Enabled Call Center

Cursor clicks the button, Star Headset comes into the foreground.

Network View: The call path goes from the airport to IP network and to the right to the Call Center.

> CALL CENTER:
> Thank you for calling Kaylee Industries. How may I help you?
>
> NARRATOR:
> With Centrex Unlimited's Internet Enabled Call Centers from Nortel Networks, there are many ways to receive prompt, reliable service. Supporting Email, POTS, and IP calls, Nortel Networks' Call Centers provide the tools to carriers, businesses and end users that enable anytime anywhere communication.

The audio ends. Two buttons appear at the bottom of the screen.
- View example without Centrex Unlimited **(T5_wo)**
Return to Desktop **(DESKTOP)**

IC2 – Incoming call 2
This is the call at the end of the sequence that rewards you with a first class ticket
(if you've beat the clock).

> Secretary:
> Great news Bob. I not only confirmed your Hotel in the Bahamas, but upgraded you to first class! Have a great trip.

IC3 – Incoming call 3
This call comes in if you've taken too much time. You've missed your plane and have an overnight layover.

> Secretary:
> Bob, I just checked with the gate and they couldn't hold your seat any longer. Also that blows the window for your suite reservation in the Bahamas. Looks like you're stuck there tonight. Sorry.

Wrap Up

After the final incoming call the user is presented with a choice to restart the simulation, view the network diagram, or return to the simulation space main menu.

Chapter 19: It's a Wrap

It's been a little over 20 years since I first seriously started making videos and films. A great deal has changed in that time, especially in terms of equipment, workflows, and competition. But there are some things that remain the same. In particular, it's the art of telling a story that is unchanged. It's still critical to be creative, make sense, hold the audience's attention, and deliver a level of quality to make a successful video. It doesn't matter what the topic or length of the piece is, these factors are important.

At the heart of any piece is the script. Writing that script is an experience in pure creative flow. When the flow is good, it's a joy to write, but when it's bad, it's bad. One trick I've used when I have a script I must create but am having a tough time getting started, is to start with nonsense. I can construct an absurd situation and then branch from it. Sometimes it might end up being in the final piece, and sometimes it may end up in the trash can. In either case, it's the getting started that's important. Similarly, when I'm starting a production with a crew, I try to get the first shot off as quickly as possible. The longer you wait, the harder it is. So once that shot is in the can, the inertia starts working for you.

When I shot my feature film Immortal, most of the first day was reshot on the last day. It turned out that getting the ball rolling cost us some footage, time and money, but it was worth it just to put the team in motion, working together, solving problems, establishing a pace, and taking everyone's mind off the fact that we were *going* to make a movie. It created the sense that we were making a movie.

Of all the ideas in this book, I think that might be the most important one. Just do it. Jump right in and start writing, start shooting, starting editing. The act of starting is the biggest teacher of all. From there it's just an exercise in keeping up with the beast you have created, keeping one step ahead of the huge boulder rolling down the hill behind you. It's hard work, frustrating, and stressful, but occasionally you'll get a nice little reminder why you wanted to do it in the first place. It can be the most fun you'll ever have.

As I started putting this book together I had a similar trepidation that I have right before a production. Where to start? Will it be any good? Will it hold an audience? I hope I've succeeded. I hope I can provide even a little inspiration to a new writer or producer. We'll see.

277

Epilogue: Chewbacca

Life at VisionFactory was often a deadline driven exercise. Like all businesses we had periods of feast and famine. We were thrilled when the work came, but it brought many challenges including long hours, limitations of processors and memory, writer's block, editor's block and so on. Two things were nice fallbacks when things got tough. First was the incredible team of creative people that we had assembled. The wide range of personalities and skillsets somehow found a way to combine into something big, a well-oiled media machine. It really was a vision factory, converting client needs into innovative media.

The second thing we had was Chewbacca.

I had a tendency not to shave when we were working on a long project. I thought of it as a chore, and sometimes I'd work $150 or so extra into a proposal budget if I need I'd have to shave for a client meeting. Since some of these projects would combine for a few 80 to 90 hour weeks in a row, my facial hair would become fairly pronounced. This combined with an occasional loud growl that emanated from the edit suite earned me the nickname Chewy. I embraced the moniker which replaced my earlier nickname "The Human Mule" which I had earned from our CEO for my tendency to pull an all-nighter edit marathon when it was most required. The Star Wars culture at VisionFactory was pervasive. Most of us had grown up on the films, and for many of us Chewy was a favorite character.

Most of the media we created was built in layers. Rarely was there simply a full frame of video. The layered approach was an outgrowth of the software we used and the products we marketing, and it became a differentiator for the company at a time wheb clients were looking for more "wow" in their product marketing. Sometimes a video would have hundreds of elements that all came together in After Effects or in a 3D render. This was complex work and could become a little maddening after several hours wrestling with a computer mouse.

Here's where Chewbacca came in. At some point I found that it was very easy to slip the image of Chewy into one of these many layers on a project. It may have been of a few frames or in an isolated corner that only I would know about, but I took limitless satisfaction that Chewy made the cut. Once, on the Unisys CBC walkthrough, our LightWave Animator Eric Jones was rendering a pass through a work area featuring a countertop with a fax machine. The smooth dolly through the virtual space was part of a much bigger, seamless sales pitch. But if you look closely as the shot plays, right on the fax machine a small sheet of paper slides out of the fax machine. Mapped onto this small virtual piece of paper is our old friend Chewbacca.

Writing about experiences that took place many years ago brings back fond memories of times that were much harder than they seem now. It's nice to know that when things got toughest, the Wookie made it better.

CPSIA information can be obtained
at www.ICGtesting.com
Printed in the USA
LVHW101916071220
673555LV00039B/1792